Simple Vegetarian Pleasures

JEANNE LEMLIN

Quill

An Imprint of HarperCollins*Publishers*

First Quill edition published 2000.

Designed by Ph.D

....

The Library of Congress has catalogued the hardcover edition as follows:

Lemlin, Jeanne.

Simple vegetarian pleasures / Jeanne Lemlin. — 1st ed.

p. cm.

Includes index.

ISBN 0-06-019135-X

1. Vegetarian cookery. I. Title.

TX837.L448 1998

641.5'636—dc21   97-43360
....

ISBN 0-06-093246-5 (pbk.)

00 01 02 03 04 ❖/RRD 10 9 8 7 6 5 4 3 2 1

I am so fortunate to have two great sisters, Jackie Lemlin and Julianne Lemlin-Dufresne

It is to them that this book is lovingly dedicated

In cooking, as in all the arts, simplicity is the sign of perfection.
— Curnonsky

The greatest dishes are very simple dishes.
— Escoffier

Simple Vegetarian Pleasures

Also by Jeanne Lemlin

Main-Course Vegetarian Pleasures

Quick Vegetarian Pleasures

Vegetarian Pleasures: A Menu Cookbook

Contents

Acknowledgments

More than any of my previous titles, this work has depended on the kindness of many people—none of them strangers.

To help conceptualize this book, I have been fortunate to exchange ideas, visions, and dreams with a number of friends who helped me in more ways than they know. My heartfelt gratitude goes to my editor, Susan Friedland, who makes me laugh, feel appreciated, and gives me room to maneuver; Lisa Ekus, my publicist, who is generous with her warmth, wisdom, and support; Darra Goldstein, whose insight and judgment I greatly value; Susan Lescher, my agent, who helped launch this book; and Nach Waxman of Kitchen Arts and Letters, for his astute observations and help with the title. Special thanks to my friends in Great Barrington, who have given me invaluable support: Jane Walsh, who shares my passion for cooking and loves to "talk food"; Geri Rybacki, whose enthusiasm for discovery has inspired me many a time; Jean Whitehead, who encouraged me to keep focused on quick cooking; Elisabeth Rhodes, who helped me with culinary history; and Debbie Reed and the staff at the Bookloft, who supply me with precious tidbits about the book industry and loyally promote me whenever they can. To the women at BCC, who have helped me tame that computer when I swore it was a Goliath: Becky Couch and Patti White, two teachers whose patience and expertise make them two in a million; and Cathy Dargi and Phylene Farrell, who generously made me feel welcomed. A special thanks to Alan Wallach of Interlaken Computers, who kept my laptop—and peace of mind—in good shape.

My family has bestowed on me much love and support. I want to especially thank my husband, Ed Curtin, for his fine judgment in critiquing dishes and his editorial skills; my son, Daniel, for his unbridled enthusiasm for the dessert chapter; my stepdaughter, Susanne, for her growing interest in using my recipes to cook for her college friends; and my mother and two sisters, for their encouragement, humor, and love of excellent vegetarian food.

Introduction

The Pleasures of Simplicity

There is a reason why the call to simplify our lives is echoed throughout modern history, and that is because chosen simplicity is inextricably linked to *enjoyment*. This, many of us are grateful to learn, is no less true in the kitchen. What a wonderful realization when we discover that a simplified approach to cooking can actually heighten the pleasures we derive from preparing food. Complex, labor-intensive recipes are welcome when the cook has time to play leisurely in the kitchen, but for the busy person who is juggling armloads, simplified cooking is essential.

How do we learn to cook quickly so that it reflects simplicity at its highest form, that is, the delivery of intensely flavored, yet uncomplicated food, rather than fare that is dull and uninspired, though also simple? We must develop a new orientation in the kitchen so that a little advance planning will take us a long way. Everyday cooking is most successful and enjoyable when it arises out of some organization. If you don't want to rely on frozen or packaged convenience foods, and you have a busy schedule, then you'll benefit tremendously by developing some new habits to make your time in the kitchen easier and more productive. Practicing the simple art of "thinking ahead" will transform your cooking. Let's examine some key elements that I have learned are crucial to creating a new strategy for simplified, sophisticated meals.

Selecting Recipes

Before you do your grocery shopping, choose a few recipes that you'd like to prepare in the upcoming week. What are you in the mood to eat? What's in season? Is there a new food that you'd like to become familiar with? Do you anticipate company coming? Will you need some do-ahead meals or would last-minute preparations suit you better? I highly recommend that you often include soup as one of your weekly choices. It's a helpful strategy to make the soup on the weekend when you have some extra time, and then reach for it on an evening when putting some heat under a pot is about all you can manage.

Make a note of the recipes that you select and hold on to it. It will be invaluable when you put together your shopping list, and will be a reminder of what you are equipped to cook throughout the week. It's a great feeling to approach a recipe and know you have everything you need.

The Shopping List

Although it can be fun and prudent to shop by spontaneously selecting what's in season or on sale, or by what grabs your attention, the shopping list is, without a doubt, salvation for the busy cook. I always have a running list on my counter so that I can immediately jot down an ingredient that I need or must replace. Shortly before I go shopping I select a few recipes for the week (as I have described above), and add those ingredients to the list. Refer to the items in "A Well-Stocked Kitchen" (opposite), and include any staples that are missing from your pantry. Now you have a truly useful shopping list, and you'll soon see how much easier this will make your cooking.

What's for Dinner

With some recipes for the week and all the ingredients you need to prepare them, you are left with the not-so-onerous task of choosing what you want each day for dinner. Don't wait until late in the day or when you come home from work to make this decision; settle this early in the morning or even the night before. Cultivating this habit will relieve you of pressure throughout the day because you'll know dinner has been decided, and you have all you need to create it. It might seem awkward at first to be thinking of dinner while you are eating breakfast, but you'll soon see how much you'll benefit from this advance planning.

Furthermore, if you can complete one recipe-related task before you leave the house in the morning, you'll be so appreciative when you return. It's amazing how just chopping a few vegetables, washing greens, cooking some rice (which takes 2 minutes of your attention and can be cooking while you're eating breakfast), or grating some cheese can significantly lessen your load at dinnertime.

Keeping Track

Have you ever prepared a fabulous recipe a few times and then, not too long thereafter, forgotten about its very existence? It's easy to lose track of old favorites when you enjoy experimenting and discovering new dishes.

To easily remember these treasures, keep an updated list of quick recipes that you love (and note where each one can be found), and tack this list to the inside of a cabinet or onto your refrigerator, or anywhere else you can easily read it. When you are making your shopping list or are in need of an idea for a quick meal, refer to your list and you'll be pleased to remember these old friends.

A Well-Stocked Kitchen

The items on this list are basic to the well-supplied kitchen and are easy to store. Do strive to keep these ingredients on hand; they will make your meal planning much easier.

On nights when you don't have a particular recipe planned, you can reach into your pantry and create an impromptu meal. Nonperishable items and those that have a long refrigerator life are easy to keep stocked because they require no attention. So refer to this itemization when you make your shopping list and you'll find it will significantly simplify your meal planning.

Cupboards or Pantry

- vegetable oil
- olive oil
- oriental sesame oil
- vinegars (red wine, balsamic, Chinese rice wine, apple cider)
- assorted pastas
- roasted red peppers
- canned plum tomatoes
- tomato sauce
- tomato puree
- tomato paste
- canned beans (chickpeas, black beans, kidney beans, small white beans)
- salsa
- lentils (brown and red)
- oats (regular and quick)
- cornmeal
- couscous
- bulghur
- rice (converted white, brown, Arborio)
- peanut butter
- unbleached flour
- sugar (white and brown)
- honey
- baking powder
- baking soda

onions (yellow and red)

garlic

Refrigerator

powdered vegetable stock base

celery

carrots

lemons

parsley

olives

whole wheat flour

tamari soy sauce

Parmesan cheese

Cheddar cheese

feta cheese

Monterey Jack cheese

nuts (almonds, walnuts, pine nuts, and pecans)

gingerroot

Freezer

peas

corn

chopped spinach

ravioli

tortellini

pita bread

tortillas

Health Issues for the Vegetarian

I have been a vegetarian for nearly 30 years and, consequently, have followed many health issues, both the benefits and pitfalls, related to maintaining a vegetarian diet.

What I have concluded after reading numerous scientific studies, hearing many unfounded claims, using common sense, and heeding my own physiological messages is that the challenge of adopting a sound vegetarian diet has been grossly exaggerated. If we eat a wide variety of foods, that is, plenty of fresh vegetables, fruits, grains, and legumes, and go easy on fats (dairy products) and sugar, then it would be virtually impossible not to thrive on a vegetarian diet. It is also crucial to acknowledge that diet is not the only factor in achieving good health; exercise and emotional well-being are key elements as well. It's a mistake to overemphasize the role food plays in making us healthy while underplaying those salient considerations.

It is my hope that after reading about the nutritional issues outlined below, you will learn to *relax* about keeping a vegetarian kitchen, and begin to *enjoy* a diet rich in plant foods. If you always bear in mind that "variety" is the one indispensable feature of a sensible meatless regimen, you will have grasped the crux of the matter and will now be able to focus on having fun cooking with these diverse ingredients.

Protein and Calcium: The Hidden Link

The number one dietary concern that has been inextricably linked to vegetarianism over the years has been adequate protein consumption. No other question has been asked of vegetarians more than "What do you do for protein?" But is there a real danger of not getting sufficient protein, or is it a pseudo concern?

America's love affair with protein, and especially meat-based protein, is a relatively recent trend. Up until 1900, 70 percent of our protein was derived from plants and 30 percent from animals. Today those figures are reversed. We all grew up with admonitions to eat enough protein, so much so that protein and health have almost become synonymous. Not only have we been told to get enough protein but to get our protein from meat. This advice seems to have been grossly off-target. Many recent studies have shown that Americans now eat twice the amount of protein they need, and that too much protein is linked to "diseases of affluence," that is, heart disease, cancers, and diabetes. This is also true for Europeans and increasingly the Japanese.

Another very interesting correlation that has recently come to light is the link between high protein intake and the loss of calcium from the bones. Calcium is an important health concern, especially for menopausal and postmenopausal women, because of the high incidence of osteoporosis in our society. Now here's where it becomes very interesting. People in many Asian and African countries, where lactose intolerance is common, consume relatively few dairy products and eat a small percentage of meat, yet have *low* rates of osteoporosis. North American and northern European populations, known to have dairy and protein-rich diets, have the greatest number of hip fractures in the world (the way we measure osteoporosis). Protein and calcium intake are high, yet as a society we have weak bones. What is going on here?

Numerous studies have suggested that excessive protein consumption may create a potentially dangerous level of urea in the blood. Minerals, including calcium, are then leached out into our urine in order for the body to rid itself of this imbalance. Osteoporosis thus appears to be a disease of excess, not deficiency. The central issue now becomes one of preventing calcium loss rather than increasing calcium intake. Avoiding a high-protein, meat-centered diet and substituting a vegetable-filled, high-fiber regimen along with vigorous daily exercise seems to be the wisest approach.

Note: For further reading on the protein/calcium connection, I'd like to refer you to two books that I have found extremely illuminating: May All Be Fed *by John Robbins (William Morrow, 1992) and* The Vegetarian Way *by Virginia Messina, M.P.H., R.D., and Mark Messina, Ph.D. (Crown Trade Paperbacks, 1996).*

Watch Those Fats

The other dietary issue that is in the foreground of vegetarianism is fat intake. Many vegetarians used to think that eliminating meat allowed us to eat liberal amounts of cheese, cream, nuts, and other high-fat foods without worry. Now we know that those fats can be just as threatening to our health, and we must watch our consumption of fat from non-meat sources as well.

I have always resisted a nutritional breakdown of recipes because I think it is counterproductive. We should be informed about which foods are high in fats and which are not, and then learn to balance our eating habits by choosing lower-fat foods the majority of time. We know when we've had rich food, and the sensible reaction is to take it easy on fats for a while. By learning to balance our eating habits this way, we never feel deprived or at war with food. Once we start calculating everything and turn our kitchens into veritable laboratories, then certain foods become forbidden and the battle begins. It's a fight few people win, I'm afraid. Success with weight control and health are much more likely when we eat good food consistently, enjoy what we eat, and adopt these habits as part of our daily life.

This relaxed approach to maintaining a healthful vegetarian diet might seem surprisingly general to those looking for detailed guidance; however, it is meant to demystify the kitchen once meat is removed from our meals so that we can approach vegetarianism with less fear.

It is important to learn about nutrition in a broad sense, e.g., good plant sources of protein, calcium, and iron, and to be aware of which foods are rich in key nutrients, but beyond that our time in the kitchen is best spent learning to cook with a diverse array of vegetables, grains, beans, and fruits, and to have fun doing so. Again, the more variety we embrace, the better off we will be.

Protein-Rich Foods

- beans and legumes
- dairy products (preferably low-fat)
- grains (especially wheat, oats, and buckwheat)
- tofu
- tempeh
- nuts
- seeds (sunflower and sesame)
- eggs

Calcium-Rich Foods

- dairy products (preferably low-fat)
- fortified soy milk
- sesame seeds and tahini
- tofu
- dark green vegetables: broccoli, kale, collards, turnip greens

Iron-Rich Foods

- seeds (sunflower and sesame)
- beans and legumes
- dried fruits
- tofu
- eggs
- raw oats
- molasses
- bran

The Basics

About Vegetable Stocks

There is probably nothing more important in the vegetarian's cache of staple ingredients than good vegetable stock, but acquiring it can be very frustrating for the busy cook. Vegetable stock is the foundation of soups, sauces, and many grain dishes such as risottos, polentas, and pilafs, and its savoriness, or lack thereof, can make or break a recipe.

I have provided a few favorite vegetable stock recipes below for the cook who has time to make these wonderful broths, but I think it would be presumptuous and unfair to expect the average person who works outside the home to have homemade stock on hand all the time. I have found a great-flavored, powdered vegetable stock base that I use when I don't have a homemade batch available (more often than not, I'll admit), and it passes my test, which is: If it's delicious enough to drink on its own, then it will be good enough for your recipe. The brand I use is Morga Vegetable Broth Mix. It's made in Switzerland, it's additive-free, and it has a wonderful flavor. There are also canned and frozen vegetable stocks available, but keep an eye on their ingredients—you don't want them to be filled with artificial flavors or preservatives.

Vegetable Stock

Here is an all-purpose vegetable stock with a light, pleasant flavor. These vegetables work well together, but others such as leeks, cauliflower, cabbage, red bell pepper, and zucchini could be included with good results. Stronger-flavored vegetables like turnips, broccoli stalks, fennel, and Swiss chard can enhance your stock, but bear in mind you should use these with a light hand so they don't dominate the final result.

Makes 7 cups

1 tablespoon olive oil
6 garlic cloves, roughly chopped
3 onions, roughly chopped
6 mushrooms, roughly chopped
3 celery ribs, roughly chopped
3 unpeeled carrots, roughly chopped
1 potato, scrubbed and diced
2 cups roughly chopped parsley (stems included)
2 bay leaves
2 tablespoons tamari soy sauce
10 cups water
Freshly ground pepper

1. Heat the oil in a large stockpot over medium heat. Add the garlic, onions, and mushrooms and sauté 10 minutes, stirring often.
2. Add all the remaining ingredients and bring the stock to a boil. Reduce the heat to a simmer and cook 1 hour, stirring occasionally. Strain the stock through a large strainer or colander set over a large bowl, and with the back of a spoon, press out as much liquid as possible from the vegetables. Discard the vegetables. Let the stock cool to room temperature, then store in the refrigerator for up to 1 week, or the freezer for up to 3 months.

Tomato-Scallion Stock

This light broth is excellent with soups that contain tomato and with risottos that are laced with spring vegetables. The tomato flavor is subtle, so it won't overpower other flavors.

Makes 7 cups

1 tablespoon olive oil

4 garlic cloves, chopped

10 scallions, chopped

2 ¼ cups (6 ounces) chopped mushrooms

2 carrots, unpeeled and chopped

2 celery ribs, chopped

1 (16-ounce) can tomatoes, chopped with their juice

10 cups water

½ teaspoon salt

Liberal seasoning freshly ground pepper

1 sprig fresh thyme, or ½ teaspoon dried

1 bay leaf

½ cup chopped fresh parsley (stems included)

1 sprig fresh marjoram, or ¼ teaspoon dried

1. Heat the oil in a large stockpot over medium-high heat. Add the garlic and scallions and cook 1 minute. Stir in the mushrooms, carrots, and celery and sauté 5 minutes, stirring often.

2. Add all the remaining ingredients and bring to a boil. Reduce to a simmer and cook 45 minutes. In batches strain the stock through a sieve, or place a colander over a large bowl and strain. With a large spoon press out all the liquid from the vegetables. Discard the vegetables. Cool completely. Refrigerate until needed for up to 1 week. If after a week you still have some stock, bring it to a boil and simmer 10 minutes. You will now be able to keep it 1 more week. Alternatively, this stock can be frozen up to 3 months.

Mushroom Stock

This stock is richly infused with the essence of mushrooms and is wonderful with risottos, pilafs, and mushroom-based soups.

Makes 8 cups

1 tablespoon olive oil
4 garlic cloves, chopped
2 onions, quartered
4 ½ cups (¾ pound) chopped mushrooms
2 carrots, unpeeled and chopped
2 celery ribs, chopped
1 tomato, cored and chopped
11 cups water
1 bay leaf
1 sprig fresh thyme, or ½ teaspoon dried
½ cup chopped fresh parsley (stems included)
½ teaspoon salt
Liberal seasoning freshly ground black pepper

1. Heat the oil in a large stockpot over medium-high heat. Add the garlic, onions, mushrooms, carrots, and celery and cook, stirring often, until the vegetables begin to brown, about 10 minutes.

2. Stir in all the remaining ingredients and bring to a boil. Reduce to a simmer and cook gently for 45 minutes.

3. In batches strain through a sieve, or place a colander over a large bowl and strain the stock. Use a large spoon and press out all the liquid from the vegetables. Discard the vegetables. Cool the stock completely. Refrigerate the stock until needed for up to 1 week. If you have any stock remaining after a week, bring it to a boil, then simmer it for 10 minutes. Now you can keep the stock 1 more week. Alternatively, freeze the stock up to 3 months.

Crostini

(Crisp Toasts)

Sometimes a basic, plain crostini is just the right vehicle for an assertive topping that might otherwise pale when spread on crackers. I prefer to use cheap, light, supermarket French bread or grinder rolls for crostini because chewy, good-quality baguettes oftentimes make hard crostini that threaten to break your teeth. Do a comparison and you'll readily see how the airiness of commercial French bread becomes an asset when toasts are created from bread you might otherwise avoid.

Makes about 20 toasts

½ narrow loaf French bread (about ¼ pound), or 2 grinder rolls
¼ cup olive oil

1. Preheat the oven to 350 degrees. With a serrated knife slice the bread into ¼-inch-thick slices. Using a pastry brush very lightly brush each side of the bread with some olive oil. Place the bread on a baking sheet in one layer.
2. Bake 5 minutes, turn each slice over, bake about 5–7 more minutes, or until lightly golden all over. Cool completely before storing in a plastic bag or tin. If stored in a refrigerator, they will keep at least 1 week.

Cooking Beans

Although I'm in favor of using canned beans when I'm pressed for time (I buy a brand made by a manufacturer that doesn't overcook its beans, and I rinse them thoroughly in a strainer before using them), cooking dry beans from scratch is, undoubtedly, the most economical and savory way to add beans to your meal planning.

It's not that cooking beans demands any skill of the cook (nothing could be easier), it's that you must think ahead if you want cooked beans to be available when you need them for a recipe. That's the hard part for most busy cooks.

If you've jumped that hurdle and are ready to cook a pot of beans, you won't regret having a batch in the refrigerator to use throughout the week. They can be marinated in a vinaigrette and used as a salad, or used in dips, in soups, with pasta, or in gratins. (See the Index under "Beans.")

Here's how you do it: Rinse the dry beans in a strainer and finger through them to locate any stones or other foreign particles. Now you can either put them in a pot and cover them with water (about 3 inches above the bean line), then let them soak overnight at room temperature, or you can use the quick-soak method: Bring the mixture to a boil and cook it 2 minutes, then let it soak (covered) for 1 hour. Both procedures will bring you to the same point—presoaked beans. Now you'll be ready to cook them.

Drain off all the soaking liquid and cover the beans with fresh, cold water to 3 inches or so above the beans. (Discarding the soaking liquid will help you digest the beans more easily.) If you like, you can flavor the cooking water with a bay leaf and a whole small onion. Bring the pot to a boil, then reduce the heat to a simmer. Cook, uncovered, until the beans are tender—this can take from about 60 minutes for small black beans or white navy beans, to 1 ½ hours for chickpeas. (Skim off any foam that rises during cooking.) I always taste the beans at various points to check on their tenderness. You don't want them at all mushy; however, they should be cooked throughout, that is, not "crunchy." When the beans are done, drain them of any remaining liquid, then let them come to room temperature. Store them in a covered bowl in the refrigerator.

Washing and Storing Greens

Assorted greens have become such a bedrock of the vegetarian and semi-vegetarian diet—whether raw in salads or cooked in soups, casseroles, or sautés—that it is imperative that we know how to properly clean and handle them.

There is really only one way to thoroughly rid these leafy gems of hidden dirt and sand, and that is by dunking them in copious amounts of cold water. Greens cannot be properly cleaned in a colander or the basket of a salad spinner; particles of grit remain lodged when rinsed this way.

Here's how to do it the right way: Fill a large pot or the base of a salad spinner with plenty of cold water. Remove the stems or cut off the core of your vegetable (depending on whether it's individual leaves or a head of something like lettuce or radicchio). Drop the leaves in the cold water and move them around with your hands. The dirt will fall to the bottom. Now here's the decisive moment: Do *not* pour the water out while the greens are in the container, or else you'll get them dirty again. Remove the greens with your hands *before* the water is dumped out, and place them in a colander or the basket part of your salad spinner. Get rid of the dirty water. Repeat this procedure a few more times, or until the soaking water is no longer dirty. You can now shake the washed greens dry in a colander, or preferably spin them in a salad spinner. If these greens are intended for a salad, then you'll have to spin them to get them sufficiently dry.

Washed greens do not store well and therefore you should clean them on the day you plan to use them. However, if you must do this step the day before you plan to work with them, the best way to store them is to roll them up in a linen kitchen towel and place the towel in the refrigerator. If you don't have a suitable towel on hand, you can place some paper towel in the bottom of a plastic bag, then put in half of the greens, then another layer of paper towel, then the remaining greens, finally ending with some paper towel. This method will also absorb any excess water clinging to the leaves, which could promote rapid decay.

Some vegetables are a lot dirtier than others. Boston lettuce, spinach, basil, leaf lettuces, and escarole harbor nuggets of dirt; whereas kale, mustard greens, and Swiss chard are relatively easy to clean. Get to know the peculiarities of different greens and handle them accordingly. There's nothing like biting into some particles of sand to ruin your meal. Once you develop a good technique for cleaning them, you'll find you can prepare leafy vegetables quite quickly and efficiently.

Roasting Peppers

Rather than roasting peppers whole, I have found that it is much easier if you cut peppers in half vertically, remove the seeds and fibrous membranes, then lay them skin side up on a baking sheet. Place an oven rack as close to the broiling element as possible, then broil the peppers until charred all over. Put the peppers in a bowl and cover the bowl with a plate or plastic wrap to trap the steam, or place the peppers in a paper or plastic bag and close tightly. Let the peppers sit 10 minutes. It is easiest to remove the skins from the peppers by peeling them in the sink under gently running water. Don't worry; this will not wash away their flavor. Pat the peppers dry with some paper towel before you proceed with your recipe.

Making Fresh Bread Crumbs

There are, undoubtedly, some instances when using commercial bread crumbs is acceptable. It is a convenience that I allow myself when the results will not be affected by the consistency of these dry, fine crumbs. However, there are also times when the success of a recipe hinges upon freshly made, coarse bread crumbs (as in Spaghettini with Garlic, Hot Peppers, and Toasted Bread Crumbs, page 239), and no substitution will do.

Tear slices of bread and process them in a food processor until they become coarse crumbs. The longer you process them the finer they become, so keep an eye on them. Certain dishes, such as the pasta dish mentioned above, require *coarse* crumbs because of their preferred texture, so you don't want to process them too long. Some recipes call for toasted fresh bread crumbs. The only difference here is that you toast the bread before you process it.

In my freezer I always keep a bag of white bread slices that are odds and ends from different loaves, and make bread crumbs as I need them; however, you can make the crumbs in advance and freeze those so that they'll be ready when you want them.

Although I generally prefer to make bread crumbs in a food processor, you can get satisfactory results with a blender. Again, just keep an eye on them.

Breakfast Is Ready

You don't need to spend hours creating a tempting breakfast table. One homemade item, such as muffins or scones, can be extended by the addition of fresh berries in season, or a simple fruit salad, and a steaming pot of perfectly brewed coffee or tea. If you choose to make French toast or pancakes, something as simple as grapefruit or a perfectly ripe melon is a fitting addition and barely increases your time in the kitchen. Perhaps you would prefer to focus on creating a glorious fruit salad; in that case, supplement it with some freshly made, store-bought bagels and you will have a well-rounded, delicious breakfast that will be relaxing for all.

See also: Frittatas and Omelets, pages 167–85

Crispy French Toast

I am indebted to my mother for a trick she learned years ago for making French toast with a crispy exterior: Coat it in flour. This produces a crust-like surface when the slices cook, and simultaneously preserves a moist interior. Children love this French toast because its texture is less eggy than the traditional variety.

Serves 4

4 large eggs
1 teaspoon cinnamon
2 cups milk
1 tablespoon vanilla extract
1 tablespoon rum, or 1 $^1/_2$ tablespoons sugar
Oil for frying
8 slices good-quality white loaf bread, or 12 slices French bread, cut 1 inch thick on the diagonal
$^1/_2$ cup unbleached flour (approximately)

1. In a large bowl whisk the eggs and cinnamon together. Whisk in the milk, vanilla, and rum. Pour this mixture into an 8 × 8-inch pan or similar medium-size shallow dish. Place a baking sheet in the oven, then preheat the oven to 250 degrees.

2. Pour a thin layer of oil into a large skillet and heat it over medium heat until hot but not smoking.

3. Place another baking sheet on the counter next to you. One by one dip the bread slices in the egg mixture and let them soak 30 seconds or so, or just until moistened. Flip over and soak again. Carefully remove the bread, letting any excess liquid drip off. Place the soaked bread in two rows on the baking sheet. Place the flour in a sieve. Shaking the sieve, sprinkle flour evenly over the bread slices. With a spatula, flip the bread over, then coat this side with flour.

4. Cook 2 slices at a time in the skillet until golden brown and crispy, about 5 minutes, then flip over and cook on the second side until golden. Keep the cooked slices hot in the oven on the baking sheet until you are ready to serve them. Continue with the remaining bread, being certain to oil the skillet in between batches. Serve with warm maple syrup.

Overnight Breakfast Casserole

No one would describe this quiche-style breakfast dish as low-fat; however, everyone will want to come back for seconds.

My sister Julianne introduced me to the idea of this delectable casserole, and I now make it two different ways. Both versions are great. The first interpretation has a bacon flavor from the inclusion of smoked tempeh strips that can be purchased in natural foods stores. These look like bacon and are cooked in a similar way. The final result of this version is reminiscent of bacon and eggs (or quiche Lorraine, I suppose). The second way I like to prepare this dish is with sautéed mushrooms, which also gives flavorful results. You choose; I'm sure you'll love both versions.

For an accompaniment, Roasted Home Fries (page 159) or Sweet Potato and Red Pepper Home Fries (page 160) are ideal. To cook them, just place the baking sheet on a lower rack in the oven (set at 350 degrees) while you bake this casserole and everything will be ready about the same time.

Serves 6

2 teaspoons canola oil

3 slices smoked tempeh strips (tempeh "bacon"), *or* 12 ounces (4 ½ cups) thinly sliced
   mushrooms

1 ½ tablespoons unsalted butter, softened

6 slices good-quality white bread

1 ½ cups grated Swiss or mild Cheddar cheese

5 large eggs

Dash nutmeg

½ teaspoon salt

1 ½ cups low-fat milk

½ cup heavy cream

1. Heat the oil in a large, preferably non-stick, skillet over medium heat. If you are using the tempeh bacon, fry it in the oil until it is golden brown on both sides. Place the strips on a plate and let cool. Cut it into ½-inch pieces. If you are using mushrooms, sauté them until their juices are rendered and then evaporated, and the mushrooms begin to brown.

2. Lightly butter a 12 × 7 × 2-inch (Pyrex) baking dish. With the 1½ tablespoons of butter, very lightly butter one side of each bread slice, then cut the bread into 1-inch cubes. Spread the cubes on the bottom of the baking dish.

3. Sprinkle the "bacon" or mushrooms on the bread cubes. Top with the grated cheese.

4. By hand or in a food processor, beat the eggs with the nutmeg and salt. Beat in the milk and cream. Pour this custard all over the bread mixture. Cover the dish and chill overnight.

5. Let the casserole stand at room temperature for 30 minutes before baking. Meanwhile, preheat the oven to 350 degrees. Bake the casserole uncovered 30–35 minutes, or until golden on top and a knife inserted in the center comes out dry. Let sit 10 minutes before cutting. As with quiche, I prefer to eat this warm, rather than piping hot.

Mixed Grain Pancakes

These scrumptious pancakes are great for breakfast or a quick, nutritious supper. The whole wheat flour and oats give them an extra boost yet still keep these pancakes light.

Serves 4

1 ¾ cups unbleached flour
½ cup whole wheat flour
¼ cup quick oats or wheat germ
2 ½ teaspoons baking powder
¼ cup sugar
1 teaspoon salt
2 large eggs, beaten
2 ½ cups low-fat milk
4 tablespoons melted butter, cooled slightly
Oil for pan

1. In a large bowl thoroughly combine the first six (the dry) ingredients.

2. In a medium-size bowl beat the eggs, then beat in the milk and butter.

3. Pour the wet ingredients into the flour mixture and stir just until evenly moistened, about 10 strokes. It's okay if there are some lumps; in fact, there should be some if you haven't overbeaten it. Let the batter rest 10 minutes.

4. Lightly oil a skillet, and heat it over medium heat until a drop of water splatters when flicked onto the pan. Pour on 2 tablespoons of batter and wait until the surface of the pancake is filled with bubbles. (Regulate the heat so the pancakes are golden underneath and covered with bubbles at the same time.) Flip and cook until golden. Serve with warm maple syrup.

Buttermilk Pancakes

Buttermilk is a tenderizer in baked goods, and in these pancakes it serves to make them light and moist. You can add blueberries to make America's favorite pancakes; just be sure to cook them throughout because they hold a tad more moisture than traditional pancakes.

Serves 3

2 large eggs

1 ½ cups buttermilk*

3 tablespoons butter, melted

1 ½ cups unbleached flour

1 ½ tablespoons sugar

1 ½ teaspoons baking powder

½ teaspoon baking soda

½ teaspoon salt

Oil for pan

1. In a large bowl thoroughly whisk the eggs. Add the buttermilk and butter and whisk until well blended.

2. Sprinkle in the flour, sugar, baking powder, baking soda, and salt and whisk just until the dry ingredients are evenly moistened. The batter will look somewhat like a yeast batter rather than standard pancake batter.

3. Pour a thin film of oil on a griddle or large skillet and heat over medium heat until a fleck of water dropped on it sizzles. Make 3-inch pancakes using a few tablespoons of batter per pancake. These won't bubble up as easily as traditional pancakes, but should have some bubbles and golden edges when they are ready to be flipped. Cook until golden brown on each side. Regulate the heat so the pancakes have time to cook throughout. Serve with warm maple syrup.

Use leftover buttermilk to make some scones (pages 32–37 in this chapter).

Summer Fruit Salad with Yogurt and Granola

This breakfast salad is the quintessential sixties dish, and has stayed around for good reason. Served with a muffin alongside it, it is one of my favorite breakfasts both at home and when traveling. The pleasing contrasts in textures and flavors and the abundance of juicy, fresh fruit make this healthful salad the ideal food with which to start the day.

Below is one of my favorite combinations of summer fruits, but peaches, blueberries, kiwis, plums, raspberries, blackberries, and honeydew melon are all wonderful additions. Just steer clear of apples and grapefruit; they clash with these delicate fruits.

Serves 4

1 small cantaloupe, diced (3 cups diced)
1 pint strawberries, each one halved
2 cups diced seeded watermelon
1 banana, thinly sliced

Yogurt Sauce
³/₄ cup plain low-fat yogurt
1 ¹/₂ tablespoons honey
Dash cinnamon

4 tablespoons granola, homemade (opposite page) or store-bought

1. Combine the fruit in a large bowl. (If you are assembling this in advance, wait until the last minute to add the banana.)
2. To make the yogurt sauce combine the yogurt, honey, and cinnamon in a small bowl. Cover and chill until ready to use, up to 24 hours ahead.
3. Just before serving divide the fruit among 4 serving bowls. Drizzle some yogurt sauce all over the top in a haphazard design. Sprinkle 1 tablespoon of granola on each serving.

Dried Cranberry and Almond Granola

Many granolas are so sweet they seem more like dessert than breakfast food. This cereal has just the right degree of sweetness, and is equally good mixed with milk or plain yogurt.

Packaged in an attractive container, Dried Cranberry and Almond Granola would be a good choice for a holiday gift.

Makes about 12 cups

½ cup canola oil
½ cup honey
6 cups oats (regular cut)
1 cup unsweetened coconut (see Note)
1 ½ cups finely chopped almonds
⅔ cup bran or wheat germ
½ cup sunflower seeds
1 tablespoon cinnamon
½ teaspoon salt
1 ¼ cups dried cranberries

1. Preheat the oven to 350 degrees.

2. In a large stockpot combine the oil and honey and heat over medium heat just until blended. Do not let it boil. Remove the pot from the heat and stir in all the remaining ingredients *except* the dried cranberries.

3. Spread one third of the granola on a large baking sheet. Bake 10 minutes. Remove from the oven and, with a spatula, toss the granola, paying special attention to the sides of the pan, which brown more quickly. Return to the oven and cook 5–10 more minutes, tossing a few more times. Do not let the granola burn; it should be a light golden brown

when done. It will get crisp when it cools. Pour the granola into a large bowl and let cool. Repeat with the remaining two batches of granola.

4. When the granola is completely cool, mix in the dried cranberries. Store in a covered container up to 3 months in the refrigerator. (You can keep a portion at room temperature during the cool-weather months, but in the summer it should be refrigerated.)

Note: Unsweetened coconut can be purchased in natural foods stores.

Muesli

Muesli is a Swiss cereal made of raw oats, dried fruit, and nuts. Admittedly, muesli isn't for everybody. Some people dislike the texture once it is mixed with milk, but I love it. I do, however, prefer to let it soak for 10–20 minutes, rather than the customary overnight soaking. It's a breeze to assemble; the only cooking involved is the toasting of the nuts. You can keep muesli at room temperature if it is in a tightly sealed container, but during the hot-weather season, you should refrigerate it.

Makes 9–10 cups

1 ½ cups finely chopped almonds or hazelnuts
3 cups regular oats
3 cups quick oats
1 cup bran
¾ cup minced dates, *or* 1 cup raisins
½ cup (1 ounce) minced dried apple (snipped with scissors)

1. Preheat the oven to 300 degrees. Spread the chopped nuts on a baking sheet and toast in the oven until lightly golden, about 5 minutes. Keep an eye on them so they don't burn. Let the nuts cool completely.
2. In a large container with a tight-fitting lid mix the nuts with all the remaining ingredients. Serve the muesli in bowls with milk and honey or brown sugar, and let sit 10–20 minutes before eating it so the mixture can soften and thicken.

Lemon–Poppy Seed Scones

Light and pillowy, these delicate scones were inspired by my reading of Phyllis Richman's *The Butter Did It*, a charming murder mystery set in the world of four-star chefs and restaurants. At one point the exhausted main character is soothed by a gift of her favorite lemon–poppy seed scones, and that sent me right into my kitchen to develop a recipe for them. The butter does it here, too.

Makes 8 scones

2 cups unbleached flour
$1/3$ cup sugar
1 tablespoon baking powder
1/2 teaspoon salt
1 tablespoon poppy seeds
5 tablespoons chilled unsalted butter
1 large egg
Grated zest of 1 lemon
2 tablespoons lemon juice
$2/3$ cup buttermilk or plain yogurt thinned with a little milk
Milk for brushing

1. Raise an oven rack to the top position in the oven. Preheat the oven to 400 degrees. Lightly butter a baking sheet and set it aside. (If you stack 2 baking sheets together you will get lighter bottoms on your scones. Invert the bottom baking sheet so that it is bottom side up, then place the baking sheet with the scones on top.)

2. In a large bowl thoroughly combine the flour, sugar, baking powder, salt, and poppy seeds.

3. Cut the 5 tablespoons butter into bits and drop them into the flour mixture. Toss to coat them, then, with the tips of your fingers or a pastry cutter, rub the butter into the flour mixture to form coarse crumbs.

4. In a medium-size bowl beat the egg. Beat in the lemon zest, lemon juice, and buttermilk. Pour this into the flour mixture and stir with a fork until the dough is evenly moistened.

5. Lightly flour your work surface. Drop the dough onto it and knead it 3 or 4 times. If it is too sticky, add a bit more flour to your work surface. Pat the dough into a disk 3/4 inch thick (no thicker), then cut it into 8 wedges (or you can cut it with a round or scalloped biscuit cutter into smaller shapes). Brush them lightly with milk to create a sheen during baking. Place the wedges on the prepared baking sheet.

6. Bake 15–17 minutes, or until golden brown. Serve warm or at room temperature, but not hot.

Oatmeal Scones

These scones are at once grainy, nubby, and tender—a wonderful combination of textures producing superior scones. Coupled with blackberry jam, they're a knockout.

Makes 8 scones

3/4 cup unbleached flour

1/4 cup whole wheat flour

1 cup quick oats, plus extra for sprinkling

2 tablespoons firmly packed light brown sugar

1 1/2 teaspoons baking powder

1/2 teaspoon baking soda

1/4 teaspoon salt

4 tablespoons unsalted butter, chilled

1 large egg

2/3 cup buttermilk or plain yogurt thinned with a little milk

Milk for brushing

1. Raise an oven rack to its highest position. Preheat the oven to 400 degrees. Lightly butter a baking sheet. (If you stack 2 baking sheets together, you will be less likely to get dark bottoms on your scones. Invert the bottom baking sheet so that it is bottom side up, then place the baking sheet that contains the scones on top.)

2. In a large bowl thoroughly combine the unbleached flour, whole wheat flour, oats, brown sugar, baking powder, baking soda, and salt.

3. Cut the 4 tablespoons butter into bits and drop them into the flour mixture. Toss to coat the bits, then, using your fingers, rub the butter into the flour mixture until coarse crumbs form, like little pellets.

4. Beat the egg in a small bowl. Beat in the buttermilk or thinned yogurt. Pour this into the flour mixture, then stir until evenly moistened.

5. Lightly flour your work surface. Dump the dough onto it and knead 3 or 4 times.

Gather the dough into a ball, then pat it into a disk $3/4$ inch thick. Cut the disk into 8 wedges. To make an attractive topping, lightly brush the top of each wedge with some milk and sprinkle on some oats, patting the oats down with your fingers to help them adhere.

6. Place the scones on the prepared baking sheet. Bake 15 minutes, or until golden brown. Serve warm or at room temperature.

Dried Cranberry–Orange Scones

The tangy, chewy character of dried cranberries is delightful in these colorful scones. Dried cranberries, also called craisins, can be purchased in most natural foods stores and specialty food shops.

Makes 8 scones

2 cups unbleached flour

$\frac{1}{3}$ cup sugar

1 tablespoon baking powder

$\frac{1}{2}$ teaspoon salt

5 tablespoons unsalted butter, chilled

$\frac{1}{2}$ cup dried cranberries

1 large egg

Grated zest of 1 orange, or $\frac{1}{2}$ teaspoon orange extract

$\frac{2}{3}$ cup buttermilk or plain yogurt thinned with a little milk

Milk for brushing

1. Raise an oven rack to its highest position. Preheat the oven to 400 degrees. Lightly butter a baking sheet and set it aside. (If you stack 2 baking sheets together, you will be less likely to get dark bottoms on your scones. Invert the bottom baking sheet so that it is bottom side up, then place the baking sheet that contains the scones on top.)

2. In a large bowl combine the flour, sugar, baking powder, and salt and mix well.

3. Cut the 5 tablespoons butter into small bits and drop it into the flour mixture, tossing thoroughly to coat the bits. With your fingers or a pastry cutter, rub the butter into the flour mixture until coarse crumbs are formed.

4. In a medium-size bowl beat the egg, then beat in the orange zest and buttermilk. Pour this into the flour mixture and stir with a large spoon just until the dough is evenly moistened.

5. Lightly flour a work surface. Drop the dough onto the flour and knead it 2 or 3 times,

or just until it is smooth. Keeping the surface lightly floured to prevent sticking, pat the dough into a 3/4-inch-thick disk, making sure it doesn't stick to the counter. Cut the disk into 8 wedges, and place them on the prepared baking sheet. Brush the scones lightly with milk.

6. Bake 15–17 minutes, or until golden brown. Serve warm or at room temperature, but not piping hot.

Preventing Burned Bottoms

Do you sometimes have a problem with keeping the bottoms of biscuits and scones from becoming too dark? If you don't have heavy-duty, high-quality baking sheets, this can be a challenge, especially with baked goods containing sugar, which will cause them to brown quicker. Even parchment paper won't prevent some scones from getting too dark.

Here are a few tricks that I have found solve the problem: When you are baking small items like biscuits and scones, raise your oven rack to its highest position; keeping the baking sheet farther from the heating element deters burning. The second thing you should do is to stack 2 baking sheets together to further insulate your baked goods. If your baking sheets are the same size, you can invert the bottom one to create a sort of platform for the top sheet. If the pan you have your biscuits or scones on is larger than your extra baking sheet, you can place the smaller one down first—right side up—and then rest the larger one on top. This will trap hot air and also shield the top baking sheet from the heating element in your oven. However you choose to do it, the idea is to add another layer of insulation that will prevent the bottom of your baking sheet from becoming too hot.

Flaky Wheat Biscuits

I used to make these biscuits only on special holidays such as Thanksgiving, but now my son requests them for breakfast, and so they have become a household staple.

You can turn these into herbed biscuits by adding a few tablespoons of minced fresh herbs to the flour mixture before you mix in the milk. The key to delicate biscuits is in a minimal handling of the dough.

Makes about 12 biscuits

1 ½ cups unbleached flour
½ cup whole wheat flour
4 teaspoons baking powder
½ teaspoon salt
5 tablespoons chilled unsalted butter
1 cup whole milk

1. Line a baking sheet with parchment paper or lightly butter the baking sheet.

2. In a large bowl thoroughly combine the two flours, baking powder, and salt. Cut the 5 tablespoons butter into bits, then toss it with the flour to coat the pieces. Using your fingers or a pastry cutter, rub the butter into the flour until coarse crumbs form. Pour in the milk and mix it into the flour just until a ball of dough can be formed. Don't overbeat.

3. Lightly flour your work surface. Drop the dough onto the surface and knead it 2 or 3 times. Pat it into a ½-inch-thick disk.

4. Using a 2-inch biscuit cutter, cut out about 12 biscuits and place them on the prepared baking sheet. Place the baking sheet in the freezer for 15 minutes, or in the refrigerator for at least 30 minutes or up to 4 hours. (Placing cold biscuits in a hot oven ensures flakiness.)

5. Meanwhile raise an oven rack to the highest position possible. Preheat the oven to 425 degrees. (If you stack 2 baking sheets together, you will less likely get dark bottoms on your biscuits—see page 37.)

6. Cook the biscuits on the top rack for 10–12 minutes, or until golden brown.

Blueberry Oat Muffins

I am not enamored of cakey blueberry muffins, but I do like them light and moist. The oats in these muffins enhance their texture and flavor so that they contain just the right balance of heft and delicacy. A sprinkling of oats and sugar on top of each muffin adds to its charm.

Makes 12 muffins

1 $\frac{1}{2}$ cups unbleached flour

$\frac{1}{2}$ cup quick oats, plus extra for sprinkling

$\frac{1}{2}$ cup sugar, plus extra for sprinkling

1 tablespoon baking powder

$\frac{3}{4}$ teaspoon salt

1 $\frac{1}{2}$ cups fresh or frozen blueberries (if frozen, unthawed, and preferably tiny wild blueberries)

1 egg

$\frac{1}{2}$ teaspoon vanilla extract

$\frac{1}{4}$ cup canola oil

1 cup low-fat milk

1. Preheat the oven to 400 degrees. Butter the insides and top of a regular-size ($\frac{1}{3}$-cup) muffin pan.

2. In a large bowl combine the flour, oats, sugar, baking powder, and salt. Add the blueberries and toss to evenly coat them.

3. In a medium-size bowl beat the egg. Beat in the vanilla, oil, and milk. Immediately pour this into the flour mixture and stir just until blended, only a few strokes.

4. Fill each prepared muffin cup with the batter. Sprinkle some oats on top of each muffin, then sprinkle on some sugar. Bake 20 minutes, or until the muffins are golden and a knife inserted in the center of a muffin comes out clean. Pop them out of the pan and cool on a wire rack. Serve warm or at room temperature.

Multi-Grain Muffins

When you want a nutrient-packed muffin that's also moist and flavorful, choose these muffins for breakfast or a snack.

Makes 12 muffins

1 ¼ cups unbleached flour

¼ cup whole wheat flour

½ cup quick oats

2 tablespoons toasted wheat germ or bran

2 tablespoons cornmeal

1 tablespoon baking powder

1 teaspoon cinnamon

½ teaspoon salt

½ cup raisins or chopped dates

¼ cup finely chopped walnuts

1 small carrot, peeled and grated

1 medium apple, peeled and grated

1 egg

½ cup canola oil

½ cup honey

1 cup low-fat milk

1. Preheat the oven to 400 degrees. Butter the tops and insides of a regular-size (⅓-cup) muffin pan.

2. In a large bowl combine all the ingredients up to and including the grated apple.

3. In another large bowl whisk the egg, oil, honey, and milk until the mixture is smooth. Mix in the dry ingredients and stir just until blended. Do not overbeat the batter. Let it sit undisturbed for 1 minute so the grains can absorb the liquid. Fill the prepared muffin cups with the batter. Bake 17–18 minutes, or until a knife inserted in the center of a muffin comes out clean. Serve warm or at room temperature, but not hot.

Banana Wheat Germ Muffins

These tender muffins are the perfect solution for overripe bananas that are too soft to eat. The riper they are, the more they'll enhance this batter.

Makes 12 muffins

1 ½ cups unbleached flour

1 cup toasted wheat germ

½ cup finely chopped walnuts

½ cup firmly packed light brown sugar

2 ½ teaspoons baking powder

¼ teaspoon ground nutmeg

½ teaspoon salt

2 large eggs

1 cup mashed ripe banana (2–3 bananas)

½ cup low-fat milk

¼ cup canola oil

1. Preheat the oven to 400 degrees. Butter the top and insides of a regular-size (1/3-cup) muffin pan.

2. In a medium-size bowl thoroughly combine the flour, wheat germ, walnuts, sugar, baking powder, nutmeg, and salt.

3. Beat the eggs in a large bowl. Beat in the mashed banana, being certain to break up any large lumps. Beat in the milk and oil until smooth. Add the dry mixture to this bowl and stir just until it is evenly moistened. Do not overbeat it.

4. Spoon the batter into the prepared muffin pan. Bake about 17 minutes, or until a knife inserted in the center of a muffin comes out dry. Cool the muffins on a rack a few minutes before serving. They are better warm, not hot.

Blueberry Almond Bread

The "almond" in this bread comes from almond extract, not chopped nuts. My son Daniel begged me not to "ruin the bread" by putting nuts in it, and so I capitulated (intending, though, to include them in the written recipe). To my surprise, he was absolutely right. The delicate, buttery texture of this marvelous bread would be compromised by the nuts, and so once again, out of the mouth of babes . . .

Makes 1 loaf

1 3/4 cups unbleached flour

1/4 cup wheat germ or bran

1 tablespoon baking powder

1/2 teaspoon salt

1 1/4 cups fresh or frozen blueberries (if frozen, unthawed, and preferably tiny wild blueberries)

6 tablespoons unsalted butter, very soft

1/2 cup sugar

2 eggs

1 teaspoon vanilla extract

1/2 teaspoon almond extract

1 cup low-fat milk

1. Preheat the oven to 350 degrees. Butter a 9 × 5-inch (1 1/2-quart) loaf pan.

2. Thoroughly combine the flour, wheat germ, baking powder, and salt in a medium-size bowl. Place the blueberries in a small bowl. Sprinkle about 2 tablespoons of the flour mixture on the blueberries and toss to evenly coat them. (This will prevent the blueberries from sinking in the batter to the bottom of the bread.)

3. Place the 6 tablespoons butter and the sugar in a large bowl. With an electric mixer beat the butter and sugar until fluffy. Beat in the eggs and vanilla and almond extracts until well blended. (It's okay if the mixture separates.)

4. Sprinkle in the flour mixture and the milk, and beat until well incorporated. *By hand* stir in the blueberries.

5. Scrape the batter into the prepared loaf pan. Bake 55 minutes, or until a knife inserted in the center of the loaf comes out clean. If the bread begins to get dark before it is finished, lay a flat piece of foil over the top and continue baking. Cool on a wire rack for 10 minutes before removing it from the pan. Let cool at least 2 hours before slicing. Do not attempt to slice this bread while it is at all warm. If well wrapped in foil and placed in a plastic bag, this bread can be frozen up to 1 week.

For Starters

The main function of hors d'oeuvres, aside from their purely pleasurable contribution, is to provide guests with some palate teasers that will gently lead them into the main meal without quelling their appetites. In addition, these nibbles allow the cook some extra time while guests chat leisurely and contentedly.

Unless the dinner is an extra-special occasion that calls for elaborate fare, I usually serve a spread of some sort, with crackers, Crostini (page 16), or pita bread triangles alongside it. This can always be extended by including olives, mini carrots, cucumbers, red pepper strips, etc., as tidbits that provide contrasting texture and color. I like to cluster individual hors d'oeuvres, such as Spinach Balls with

Honey-Mustard Dipping Sauce or Pan-Fried Ravioli with Sun-Dried Tomato Pesto, with other finger foods to create an appetizer menu. (Christmas Eve is my favorite time to do this.)

When you are going to select an appetizer to precede a carefully planned dinner, take care to match compatible flavors and ingredients. If the main course is rich with cheese, avoid a cheese-based starter. If red peppers are a salient ingredient in the entree, select an appetizer without them.

All these recipes can be prepared in advance (or at least a number of their steps can), so take advantage of this feature to enjoy your guests, and save last-minute prep time for other courses that need your attention.

Tiny Eggplant Turnovers

The idea for this hors d'oeuvre came to me one night in bed, and I couldn't wait to get up the next morning to try it out. Thin slices of breaded eggplant are spread with a goat cheese–red pepper filling and then folded over to make half moons. You could even use small Japanese eggplants and make little sandwiches instead of the turnovers, or if you can only get a large eggplant, cut each slice in half before you turn it over. Whichever method you choose, you'll find that this appetizer is addictive.

Makes about 24 turnovers

1 medium (about 1 $\frac{1}{4}$ pounds) eggplant (skin left on), sliced into $\frac{1}{3}$-inch-thick slices (no thicker)

$\frac{1}{4}$ cup mayonnaise (approximately)

$\frac{1}{3}$ cup dry bread crumbs (approximately)

$\frac{1}{2}$ teaspoon dried basil

Salt

Freshly ground pepper to taste

The Filling

5 ounces soft mild goat cheese (chèvre)

1 small garlic clove, put through a press

2 tablespoons very finely diced roasted red pepper, freshly roasted (page 19) or store-bought

$\frac{1}{2}$ teaspoon dried oregano

$\frac{1}{4}$ teaspoon dried thyme

Salt

Freshly ground black pepper to taste

Minced parsley for garnish

1. Preheat the broiler.

2. Place the eggplant slices in front of you. Put the mayonnaise in a small bowl. Mix the bread crumbs, basil, salt, and pepper together on a small plate.

3. With a pastry brush very lightly coat both sides of each eggplant slice with some

mayonnaise, then press each slice into the bread crumbs to coat it evenly. Place the slices on a baking sheet in one layer. Broil until golden brown on each side. Let the eggplant cool to room temperature. Do not fill it while it is at all warm.

4. To make the filling combine the filling ingredients in a small bowl. When the eggplant is cool spread a *thin* layer of filling on each slice. Fold the slices over to make turnovers. Arrange decoratively on a platter, then sprinkle on some minced parsley to garnish them. Serve at room temperature.

Note: You can prepare and chill these up to 24 hours in advance. Bring to room temperature before serving.

Cheesy Polenta Disks
with Assorted Toppings

Because these little disks of polenta are just the right size and firmness to be grasped easily while holding a glass of wine in the other hand, they can be a great hors d'oeuvres for a party. The bright yellow polenta lends itself to whimsical, colorful toppings. I like to use slices of plum tomatoes on some, and chopped black olives on others; however, you can try: paper-thin slices of sautéed red, green, and yellow bell peppers; sliced cherry tomatoes and capers; sautéed diced red onion; and sautéed mushrooms, just to name a few possibilities. Just be certain to place some cheese on the polenta disks before garnishing them so that the toppings will have something to adhere to.

You can also be playful with the *shapes* of these tidbits. My preference is to use a 2½-inch fluted biscuit cutter, but you can use other cutters such as hearts, ovals, diamonds, etc.

If you have a big crowd, don't hesitate to multiply this recipe; it's very easy to handle.

Serves 4

1¾ cups vegetable stock, store-bought or homemade (page 13)

¼ teaspoon salt

½ teaspoon finely chopped fresh rosemary, or ⅛ teaspoon dried, crumbled

½ cup cornmeal

1 tablespoon unsalted butter

2 tablespoons grated Parmesan cheese

½ cup grated part-skim mozzarella cheese

1 tablespoon olive oil

The Toppings

⅓ cup grated part-skim mozzarella cheese

1 plum tomato, cut into 6 thin slices

6 pitted black olives (your favorite kind), each cut into quarters

1. **Place a baking sheet in front of you to pour the polenta on. Combine the vegetable**

stock, salt, and rosemary in a medium-size, heavy-bottomed saucepan and bring to a boil. Reduce the heat to a simmer, then slowly drizzle in the cornmeal, whisking all the while with a wire whisk. Continue to whisk until the polenta tears away from the sides of the pot, about 5 minutes. Whisk in the butter, and the Parmesan and mozzarella cheeses. Pour the polenta onto the baking sheet so that it is ½ inch thick. Use a rubber spatula to spread it around evenly; it should fill about one third of the pan. Let the polenta cool. Cover it with plastic wrap, and chill for at least 30 minutes, or up to 2 days.

2. Preheat the oven to 425 degrees. Using the tablespoon of olive oil, grease a baking sheet. With a 2½-inch fluted biscuit cutter or other shape of your choice, cut out polenta disks. Lift the disks with a narrow spatula and place them on the prepared baking sheet. You should have about 12.

3. Place a teaspoon or so of the grated mozzarella on each disk. Place a slice of tomato on 6 of the disks, and the quartered olives on the other 6 disks. Bake 10 minutes, or until the cheese has melted and the disks are sizzling. Let sit 2 minutes before removing them from the pan. (They tend to stick a bit but are manageable.) Place on a decorative platter, and serve warm, not piping hot.

Pan-Fried Ravioli
with Sun-Dried Tomato Pesto

My son Daniel can't get enough of these crisp ravioli. Although I like to serve them as hors d'oeuvres, he prefers them for his main course (minus the sauce). In our house they have become a perfect quick, staple dinner to fix for our selective ten-year-old. Fresh ravioli work best with this treatment because they remain tender and delicate; however, defrosted frozen ravioli will be just fine if that's what you have on hand. For entertaining I arrange them decoratively on a platter with a tiny spoonful of pesto on top of each one.

Serves 4–6 as an hors d'oeuvre

The Pesto
1 ½ ounces (about 10) loose sun-dried tomatoes
¼ cup olive oil
2 small garlic cloves, chopped
1 tablespoon lemon juice
2 tablespoons pine nuts
½ cup chopped fresh parsley
¼ teaspoon salt
Freshly ground pepper
1 tablespoon grated Parmesan cheese

⅓ cup milk (approximately)
5 tablespoons dry bread crumbs (approximately)
20 cheese ravioli, defrosted if frozen
Oil for frying

1. To make the pesto, steam the tomatoes in a vegetable steamer until soft, about 10 minutes. Remove and let cool.
2. In a food processor combine the tomatoes, oil, garlic, and lemon juice and process until smooth. Add the pine nuts, parsley, salt, and pepper and pulse until the mixture is

almost smooth but has tiny bits of these last ingredients visible. Scrape the pesto into a small bowl, then stir in the cheese by hand.

3. To prepare the ravioli put the milk in a small bowl and the bread crumbs on a small plate and place them in front of you. Dip each ravioli in the milk, then coat both sides with bread crumbs, being careful to cover them completely. Place all the ravioli on a large plate or platter.

4. Cover the bottom of a large skillet with a little oil. Heat it over medium heat until hot but not smoking. Fry the ravioli in one layer (you'll probably have to do this in batches) until golden brown on both sides. Use tongs to flip them over as needed. Place on a paper towel–covered plate to drain. Serve on a platter with $\frac{1}{2}$ teaspoon of tomato pesto on top of each one.

Note: If there is any leftover pesto, you can cover and refrigerate it for a few days, then serve it on toasted French bread slices, on leftover pasta, in an omelet, or in a vegetable soup.

Leek Puff Pastries

For entertaining I like to cook these elegant, bite-sized puffs in advance and then reheat them a few minutes prior to serving. This method keeps the pace relaxed by eliminating any last-minute fussing. This hors d'oeuvre is not difficult or time-consuming, but you must poke the pastries a few times while they are baking. I like to get this step over with before the guests arrive.

Don't let the length of these instructions dissuade you from trying these flaky pastries; the recipe is not painstaking at all.

Makes 40 puffs

2 large leeks
1 tablespoon plus 2 teaspoons unsalted butter
¼ cup heavy cream
Two pinches dried thyme
Pinch sugar
Salt
Generous seasoning freshly ground black pepper
⅔ cup (2 ounces) grated Gruyère or other Swiss cheese
1 (17-ounce) box frozen puff pastry sheets, thawed
Flour for dusting

1. Cut the roots off the leeks plus everything but 2 inches of the green tops. Cut the leeks in half lengthwise. Under cold running water rinse the leeks, thumbing through all the leaves to wash away any hidden dirt. Thinly slice the leeks, discarding any thick, dark green pieces that look tough. You should get about 2 ½ cups sliced leeks.

2. Melt 1 tablespoon of the butter in a large skillet over medium heat. Add the leeks and sauté until very tender, about 10 minutes. Do not let the leeks get at all brown. Mix in the cream, thyme, sugar, salt, and pepper and cook just until the cream is very thick and

coats the leeks, about 3 minutes. Scrape the mixture into a bowl and let cool to room temperature. Stir in the cheese.

3. Unfold the puff pastry sheets. Lightly flour your work surface, then roll each sheet into a 10 × 10-inch square. With a 2-inch biscuit cutter cut out as many rounds as possible, probably 20 per sheet. Use your thumb to make a few indentations in the center of each round. This will cause the sides to raise up a bit, like a saucer.

4. Melt the remaining 2 teaspoons of butter. With a pastry brush lightly coat the edge of each round. Using a measuring teaspoon, place 1 teaspoon of filling in the center of each round. Place the rounds on ungreased baking sheets.

5. Now you can proceed in the following ways: Freeze the pastries for 30 minutes, then when hard, cover them with plastic wrap and cook within 1 week; or chill them up to 4 hours, then bake; or bake as directed (below) and reheat before serving.

6. To bake them preheat the oven to 400 degrees. Bake the pastries about 4 minutes, or until they begin to rise. To prevent them from toppling over, which they sometimes do if they rise too high, remove the baking sheets from the oven and, with a sharp, pointed knife, poke a few holes in the sides of the pastries to let steam escape. Return to the oven and bake 6 more minutes, or until golden, checking and poking them as necessary. Serve warm, not hot, or let cool completely, then reheat in a 350-degree oven for 4–5 minutes.

Spinach Balls with
Honey-Mustard Dipping Sauce

These tender, green morsels are very quick to prepare, and because you can freeze the balls uncooked, they are ideal for entertaining. I use frozen rather than fresh spinach here because it all gets pureed and you can't tell the difference.

Makes about 40 balls

2 (10-ounce) packages frozen chopped spinach, thawed

1 medium onion, minced

$^1\!/_2$ cup dry bread crumbs

1 teaspoon poultry seasoning

$^3\!/_4$ cup grated Parmesan cheese

6 tablespoons unsalted butter, melted

3 eggs

$^1\!/_4$ teaspoon salt

Oil for baking sheet

Honey-Mustard Dipping Sauce

$^1\!/_2$ cup plain yogurt

2 tablespoons Dijon-style mustard

4 teaspoons honey

1. Squeeze all the water out of the spinach with your hands, or by placing it in a strainer and pressing out the liquid with the back of a large spoon. Place the spinach and onion in a food processor and process until the onion is fine.

2. Stop the machine and add the bread crumbs, poultry seasoning, cheese, butter, eggs, and salt. Process until perfectly pureed. Scrape the mixture into a bowl and chill until cold, at least 1 hour.

3. Lightly oil a baking sheet. Roll the mixture into balls 1 to 1 $^1\!/_2$ inches in diameter, and place them on the baking sheet. At this point you can place the baking sheet in the refrigerator and chill the balls until you are ready to bake them, or place the baking

sheet in the freezer for about 1 hour, or until the balls are frozen. With a spatula remove the frozen balls and place them in a plastic bag. Freeze up to 1 month.

4. Preheat the oven to 350 degrees. Bake the spinach balls 10–15 minutes (unthawed if frozen), or until they are hot throughout and lightly golden. Don't overcook them or they will get dry. Serve them warm, not hot, around a bowl of Honey-Mustard Dipping Sauce.

5. To make the sauce combine the ingredients in a small bowl. Chill until ready to use.

SIMPLE VEGETARIAN PLEASURES

Caramelized Onion, Gorgonzola, and Walnut Bruschetta

I once tasted this magical combination of caramelized onion, Gorgonzola cheese, and walnuts on a pizza that was created by Joyce Goldstein, chef of the now defunct Square One restaurant in San Francisco, and I was totally captivated by the fantastic interplay of flavors. Here it is repeated on a bruschetta (grilled or toasted bread) and it retains all the charm of the original combination.

Makes 8 bruschetta

½ tablespoon unsalted butter
1 large onion, halved vertically and very thinly sliced
Pinch sugar
4 tablespoons crumbled Gorgonzola or other blue cheese
2 ½ tablespoons finely chopped walnuts
8 slices baguette, each ½ inch thick
Fruity olive oil for brushing

1. Heat the butter in a medium-size skillet over medium heat. Add the onion and, with the tip of a spoon or spatula, break the onion slices into rings. Sauté 5 minutes, tossing occasionally.

2. Add the pinch of sugar, cover the pan, and lower the heat. Cook until the onion is evenly caramelized and soft, about 15 minutes. Stir repeatedly. Scrape the onion into a bowl and let cool. Mix in the Gorgonzola and walnuts.

3. Preheat the oven to 400 degrees. Place the bread on the baking sheet and toast until golden on both sides. Lightly brush some olive oil on one side of the toast.

4. Spoon an equal portion of the Gorgonzola mixture onto the oiled side of each toast. Pat it down firmly with your fingers. (You can assemble the bruschetta up to an hour before cooking them.) Bake until hot and melted, about 7 minutes. Serve warm.

Bruschetta

(pronounced broos-KAYT-tah)

Peasant cooks worldwide have found ingenious, yet simple, uses for stale bread. That these treatments are born of necessity and frugality only adds to their rustic charm, for it is no small feat to avoid waste.

Roman peasants created bruschetta as one answer to the prevalence of stale bread. Thick slices of chewy bread are grilled over a wood fire; they are then sometimes rubbed with garlic, and always drizzled with olive oil. This is the essence of bruschetta, and from here, many offshoots extend.

For the contemporary cook, toasting often has to replace grilling if no grill is available. And bruschetta are now widely used as a base for many delectable toppings, which makes them ideal hors d'oeuvres, especially when served with some robust wine. But the two characteristics of bruschetta that must never be tampered with in order to preserve its distinctiveness are the use of chewy, crusty bread, and fruity, extra-virgin olive oil. That aside, you can have fun with endless toppings.

Triple Pepper Bruschetta

These colorful little morsels are just the thing to serve with some wine when the guests arrive. This topping is so tasty that I oftentimes use it as a sandwich filling with some sliced cheese, all atop some chewy Tuscan-style bread.

About 12 small bruschetta

2 tablespoons fruity olive oil, plus extra for brushing
$\frac{1}{2}$ red bell pepper, cut into $\frac{1}{8} \times 2$-inch strips
$\frac{1}{2}$ yellow bell pepper, cut into $\frac{1}{8} \times 2$-inch strips
$\frac{1}{2}$ green bell pepper, cut into $\frac{1}{8} \times 2$-inch strips
1 medium onion, halved vertically and very thinly sliced
1 tablespoon minced fresh basil
Salt
Freshly ground black pepper
12 slices baguette, cut $\frac{3}{4}$ inch thick

1. Heat the 2 tablespoons olive oil in a large skillet over medium heat. Add the 3 peppers and the onion and sauté, tossing often, for 10 minutes. Cover the pan and cook about 20 minutes more, or until the mixture is very soft and almost caramelized. Stir it occasionally. Remove from the heat and let cool to warm. Stir in the basil, salt, and pepper.

2. Grill or toast the bread slices until they are lightly browned. (You can toast them in a toaster or in a 400-degree oven.) Lightly brush some olive oil on each toast. Neatly arrange some of the pepper mixture on each one. Arrange the bruschetta on a decorative plate. You can let the bruschetta sit up to 20 minutes before serving them.

Spinach Dip with Pita Crisps

These sturdy crisps are just what is needed to scoop up this bulky, delectable dip.

Serves 4–6

The Dip

½ (10-ounce) package frozen chopped spinach, thoroughly defrosted (see Note)

1 cup sour cream

1 large scallion, very thinly sliced

2 tablespoons pine nuts, toasted

2 teaspoons lemon juice

1 tablespoon milk

¼ teaspoon salt

Generous seasoning freshly ground black pepper

The Pita Crisps

2 (6-inch) pita breads

2 tablespoons olive oil

1. Place the half portion of defrosted spinach in a strainer and press out *all* the liquid with the back of a large spoon. Place the spinach in a medium-size bowl. Stir in all the remaining dip ingredients. Cover and chill for at least 2 hours to blend the flavors.

2. To make the pita crisps, preheat the oven to 300 degrees. Cut both pita breads in half to make 4 pockets, then, with a small knife, carefully separate each pocket into single layers. Using a pastry brush, coat each piece of bread on the rough (inner) side with the olive oil. Cut each piece into 3 or 4 triangles.

3. Place the pita triangles on a baking sheet, then bake until golden and crisp, about 12–15 minutes. Let cool completely. Store in a plastic container until ready to use. Serve surrounding the bowl of spinach. Serve the dip cool or at room temperature, not cold.

Note: The remaining half box of spinach can be used to fill an omelet, mix with pasta, or stuff into a baked potato with some cheese.

Two White Bean Spreads

Both these spreads are teeming with flavor and are delightful spread on toasts, especially those made from French bread slices (see Crostini, page 16).

The first version is enlivened with basil and roasted red peppers, the second spread has a dominant scallion-onion theme. I had a hard time choosing which one I preferred, so I have included both.

Makes about 1 1/2 cups (each)

Spread #1

1/2 cup chopped fresh parsley

1 (16-ounce) can small white beans, rinsed well and drained

1 tablespoon olive oil

2 tablespoons finely diced roasted red peppers, freshly roasted (page 19) or store-bought

2 tablespoons minced fresh basil

1 garlic clove, put through a press

Salt

Freshly ground black pepper

Spread #2

1/2 cup chopped fresh parsley

1 (16-ounce) can small white beans, rinsed well and drained

1 tablespoon olive oil

1 garlic clove, put through a press

2 tablespoons minced scallion, white and green parts

1 tablespoon minced red onion

Salt

Freshly ground black pepper

1. **For each spread proceed in the same manner.** Place the parsley in a food processor and process until fine. Scrape it into a medium-size bowl. Don't worry about getting it

all out of the processor. Place the beans and olive oil in the processor and process until smooth. Mix the beans into the parsley.

2. In either case, whether you're making spread #1 or #2, mix in all the remaining ingredients. Cover and chill for at least 1 hour before serving so the flavors can blend. Bring to room temperature before serving.

Vegetarian Chopped Liver

The transformation of these ingredients into a sensational mock chopped liver spread is just short of magical. Spread it on room temperature toast points, preferably made from good-quality white bread.

Makes 2 ¹/₂ cups

1 cup walnuts
1 ¹/₂ tablespoons canola oil
2 medium onions, diced
2 cups (¹/₂ pound) fresh or frozen diced green beans
3 hard-boiled eggs, chopped
4 teaspoons tomato paste
2 tablespoons mayonnaise
¹/₂ teaspoon salt
Generous seasoning freshly ground black pepper

1. Preheat the oven to 350 degrees. Place the walnuts in a shallow pan and toast until fragrant and golden, about 5–7 minutes. Let cool.

2. Heat the oil in a small skillet. Sauté the onions until very tender and deep brown, about 15 minutes. Set aside to cool.

3. Steam the fresh or frozen green beans until they are very tender and begin to turn olive green in color. (You don't want bright, crunchy green beans for this recipe.) Set aside to cool.

4. In a food processor combine all the ingredients and process until perfectly smooth, almost 5 minutes of processing. Turn off the machine and scrape down the sides as necessary. Scrape into a bowl, cover, and chill at least 4 hours or up to 3 days before serving. Serve at room temperature.

Hummus

Hummus recipes are everywhere, but I can guarantee you that few are as luscious as this one. The secret is in the generous use of tahini. Tahini (sesame butter), a great non-dairy source of calcium, gives this hummus its silken consistency and rich flavor.

For busy cooks (our numbers are legion), this hummus can be a godsend, for it can be used throughout the week in a variety of ways, and this recipe makes an ample amount to provide for that. (See "Uses" below.) When company is coming it is the perfect recipe to reach for because it is so delicious and versatile, and you can prepare it well in advance. Have I convinced you to try this captivating spread? It's bound to become one of your favorites.

Makes 2 ½ cups

2 cups freshly cooked or canned chickpeas, drained and well rinsed if canned
3 garlic cloves, minced
½ cup fresh lemon juice (about 3 lemons)
1 cup tahini*
½ teaspoon salt
½–1 cup water
Paprika for garnish

1. Combine the chickpeas and garlic in a food processor and process until a mealy texture is formed. Stop the machine and add the lemon juice, tahini, salt, and ½ cup of the water. Process until very smooth and creamy, at least 2 minutes.

Tahini is sesame butter made from untoasted sesame seeds. It is different from Chinese sesame paste, which is dark and roasted. Stir the tahini well before measuring it because its oil will most likely have risen to the top.

2. Stop the machine and check the consistency. It should be like soft mashed potatoes, not thick and pasty. With the machine running add more water if necessary until it is smooth and creamy. Scrape into a bowl and garnish with some paprika. This hummus will last a week if well covered and refrigerated.

Uses for hummus:

✤ As an appetizer: Serve as a spread with hot pita triangles or Pita Crisps (page 60).

✤ For sandwiches: Place raw, crisp vegetables, such as cucumbers, peppers, Romaine lettuce, and some tomato wedges or cherry tomatoes, in pita bread halves and spoon on some hummus.

✤ Spread it on bagels.

✤ Make an open-faced sandwich by spreading hummus on whole grain bread, then topping it with some red onion, thin cucumber slices, and alfalfa sprouts.

Roasted Red Pepper Spread

I love to pipe this rosy spread onto cucumber rounds and serve them as hors d'oeuvres. It is equally delicious, though, spread on Crostini (page 16) or crackers. Whichever you choose, it will be a hit at any gathering.

Makes about 1 1/2 cups

1/2 cup roasted red peppers, store-bought or freshly roasted (page 19), patted *very* dry
1 small garlic clove, put through a press or minced*
8 ounces Neufchâtel cheese (light cream cheese), at room temperature
2 tablespoons lemon juice
Salt to taste
2 teaspoons minced fresh parsley
1 teaspoon minced fresh basil, or 1/4 teaspoon dried

1. Process the peppers and garlic in a food processor just until very finely chopped.
2. Add the Neufchâtel and lemon juice and process just until smooth. Scrape the mixture into a bowl, then stir in the salt, parsley, and basil. Cover and chill at least 1 hour.
Note: To pipe it onto cucumber rounds, place the spread in a pastry bag with a large star tube. Keeping the skin on, slice an English (seedless) cucumber into 1/4-inch-thick slices. Pat them dry with paper towels. Pipe a thick row of the spread on each slice. Garnish the top of the row with a parsley leaf.

*You must mince the garlic before adding it to the processor or else the blade could miss it and it will remain whole.

SIMPLE VEGETARIAN PLEASURES

Goat Cheese Spread with Pistachios and Mint

My friend Jane Walsh put mint in a cheese mixture once and I loved the fresh nuance it lent the spread. Here, mixed with pistachio nuts, you have an appetizer with simple elegance. After the cheese mixture is unmolded onto a platter, you can create a Moroccan theme by surrounding it with black olives, orange wedges, and raw fennel slices—all exciting and compatible flavors. Oh, and don't forget the crackers!

Serves 6

5 ounces soft mild goat cheese
2 tablespoons coarsely chopped shelled pistachio nuts
1 tablespoon minced fresh mint, or 1 teaspoon dried

1. In a medium-size bowl mash the goat cheese with a fork. Stir in the nuts and mint.

2. Line a 6-ounce custard cup or other ramekin with a piece of plastic wrap that's big enough to extend over the sides. Pack in the goat cheese mixture and smooth over the top. Fold over the plastic to cover the cheese. Chill at least 1 hour or up to 8 hours before serving. To serve, invert the cup onto a large serving plate, then remove the cup and plastic. Let the cheese come close to room temperature so that it isn't ice cold. Surround the cheese with crackers or Crostini (page 16), and perhaps some olives, sliced raw fennel, and orange slices.

Special Dinner Salads

It's easy to get into a rut serving the same salad meal after meal. When we find a harmonious combination of leafy vegetables that match well with a favorite dressing, that oftentimes becomes one course that we are grateful *not* to have to think about.

But upon further reflection, the salad course is more important than many of us imagine. It is the prelude to our meal (in the United States, at least, where it is customary to serve the salad before the entree rather than after it, as many Europeans do), and can set a tone that makes our guests or family eager to taste what will follow.

To make a memorable salad doesn't demand any more time than your everyday salad, just a good dose of imagination.

Salad of Baby Greens with Baked Goat Cheese

Here's a variation of the salad made famous at the restaurant Chez Panisse in Berkeley, California. The little rounds of creamy goat cheese encased in buttery bread crumbs are truly irresistible, and inevitably make the salad a hit at any dinner party.

Serves 4

The Dressing
1 ½ tablespoons lemon juice
2 teaspoons red wine vinegar
1 small garlic clove, minced
Salt
Freshly ground black pepper
5 tablespoons olive oil

Olive oil for greasing

The Salad
½ cup toasted fresh bread crumbs (from about 1 slice toast)
1 teaspoon chopped fresh thyme, or ¼ teaspoon dried
Salt
Freshly ground black pepper
1 (4-ounce) log soft mild goat cheese (such as Montrachet), cut into 4 rounds
8 cups mesclun (mixed baby greens)

1. Combine the ingredients for the salad dressing in a jar with a tight-fitting lid and shake vigorously. Set aside.

2. Very lightly oil the center portion of a baking sheet. Place the bread crumbs in a small bowl and mix in the thyme, salt, and pepper. Using a pastry brush or your fingers, one by one lightly coat each goat cheese round with some olive oil, then press the rounds into the bread crumbs to coat them with a thick crust. Lay them on the center portion of the baking sheet. You can cook them now, or chill them until you are ready, up to 4 hours.

3. Preheat the oven to 425 degrees. Bake the cheese until golden on the outside and hot on the inside, about 5 minutes. Keep an eye on it so it doesn't become so hot that it melts.

4. Toss the greens with the dressing. Divide them among 4 salad plates. Place 1 goat cheese round on top of each serving of greens. Serve immediately.

Goat Cheeses
(Chèvres)

A new appreciation for goat cheeses is sweeping the United States, and these once uncommon little parcels can now be found in most supermarkets. Technically chèvre refers to a French cheese made from goat's milk; Montrachet and Boucheron are two of the most well known. But the United States is now producing some wonderful goat cheeses, and it seems appropriate to drop the French designation and refer to them as "goat cheese."

Goat cheeses range in texture from soft and creamy to hard and shrunken, and in flavor from mild to strong. In this book soft, fresh, mild goat cheese is the cheese of preference when goat cheese is called for. Montrachet is the mildest chèvre from France, and the United States has many to choose from. Check your local cheese store or the cheese section of a top-notch supermarket to become familiar with what's available to you. Where I live in the Berkshires, we have wonderful goat cheese that's made locally. See if you do.

Green Leaf Salad with Fennel, Apple, and Pecans

Here's a special salad that has lots of crunch and a great variety of flavors. Because it has no cheese or dairy in it, it's a good choice for a meal that's on the rich side.

Serves 4

Balsamic Vinaigrette
2 tablespoons balsamic vinegar
1 garlic clove, put through a press or minced
¼ teaspoon salt
Freshly ground black pepper
5 tablespoons olive oil

6 cups torn-up green leaf lettuce, washed and spun dry
1 cup torn-up radicchio, washed and spun dry
½ large Granny Smith apple, cut into 12 thin slices
⅔ cup thinly sliced fennel (see Note)
½ cup chopped toasted pecans

1. Combine all the ingredients for the dressing in a medium-size bowl and whisk until blended.

2. Mix the lettuce and radicchio in a salad bowl. Just before serving pour on the dressing and toss. Divide salad among 4 salad plates.

3. Place 3 apple slices on one side of each salad, and one quarter of the fennel on the other side. Sprinkle the pecans all over the salads. Serve immediately.

Note: Leftover fennel can be used in Chickpea Salad with Fennel, Tomatoes, and Olives (page 94), or Leek, Fennel, and Goat Cheese Frittata (page 170), or Tortellini with Fennel, Tomatoes, and Spinach (page 229).

Mixed Greens with Pears, Walnuts, and Blue Cheese

This salad is so delicious that I sometimes serve double portions to create a luncheon entree. For the greens I especially love Boston lettuce and watercress to dominate, with a touch of Romaine for crunch and radicchio for color. Because it is a tad on the rich side, I like to match it with a light entree for balance when I serve it as a salad course.

Serves 4

6 cups bite-size mixed greens, such as Boston lettuce, Romaine, and radicchio

1 bunch watercress, tough stems discarded and large pieces torn in half

The Dressing

1 tablespoon lemon juice

2 teaspoons red wine vinegar

1 small garlic clove, minced

Salt

Freshly ground black pepper

5 tablespoons olive oil

1 ripe pear (preferably D'Anjou), cored and cut into 12 slices

4 tablespoons crumbled blue cheese

3 tablespoons chopped toasted walnuts

1. Wash and spin dry all the greens, then place them in a large salad bowl.

2. To make the dressing combine the lemon juice, vinegar, garlic, salt, pepper, and olive oil in a jar with a tight-fitting lid and shake vigorously.

3. Place the pear slices in a medium-size bowl, and mix with 1 tablespoon of dressing. Toss to coat evenly and prevent the pear from discoloring.

4. Pour the remaining dressing on the salad greens and toss. Divide the salad among 4 salad plates. Place 3 slices of pear in the center of each salad. Sprinkle on the blue cheese and walnuts. Serve immediately.

Mesclun Salad with
Dried Apricots and Spiced Nuts

The tiny bursts of spiciness from the nuts are a pleasing counterpoint to the sweet and tangy bits of dried apricot, together making this a superlative prelude to a special meal. The recipe might look lengthy, but it's a breeze to prepare.

Serves 4

Spiced Nuts
1 teaspoon unsalted butter
$1/4$ teaspoon chili powder
$1/4$ teaspoon ground cumin
Dash cayenne
A few dashes salt
$1/2$ cup roughly chopped walnuts

The Salad
5 cups mesclun (baby greens), washed and spun dry
5 cups torn Boston lettuce, washed and spun dry
$1/2$ cup slivered red onion
8 dried apricots, snipped with scissors into quarters

The Dressing
$1 1/2$ tablespoons balsamic vinegar
$1/2$ teaspoon Dijon-style mustard
$1/4$ teaspoon sugar
$1/4$ teaspoon salt
Freshly ground black pepper
5 tablespoons olive oil

1. To make the spiced nuts, melt the butter in a medium-size skillet over medium heat. Sprinkle in the chili powder, cumin, cayenne, and salt and, using a spatula, blend it together. Cook 1 minute. Add the walnuts, toss to coat well, and cook 3–5 minutes, toss-

ing frequently. The nuts should be toasted when done. Set aside to cool completely.

2. Combine the salad ingredients in a large salad bowl.

3. Whisk together the dressing ingredients in a small bowl until smooth and emulsi-fied, or place them in a jar with a tight-fitting lid and shake vigorously.

4. Just before serving pour three quarters of the dressing on the salad. Toss to coat well. If you need more, then add it, but be careful not to overdress the greens; they are soft and delicate. Arrange the salad on 4 salad plates, and sprinkle $\frac{1}{4}$ of the nuts on each portion.

Boston Lettuce and Arugula Salad with Dried Cranberries and Walnuts

A delicate, pretty salad that's a good choice when your meal is hearty and you want a light salad to balance it. I especially like this salad for the holidays.

Serves 4

Lemon-Soy Dressing
1 ½ tablespoons lemon juice
1 ½ teaspoons red wine vinegar
1 garlic clove, put through a press or minced
1 ½ teaspoons tamari soy sauce
Salt
Freshly ground black pepper
5 tablespoons olive oil

3 tablespoons dried cranberries
2 tablespoons chopped walnuts
6 cups bite-size pieces Boston lettuce, well washed and spun dry (from about 1 ½ heads)
2 cups torn-up arugula, washed and spun dry
1 scallion, thinly sliced

1. Combine all the ingredients for the dressing in a jar with a tight-fitting lid and shake vigorously. Place the cranberries and walnuts in a small bowl, then pour on a tiny bit of dressing to moisten them and soften the cranberries a bit.

2. Combine the salad greens and scallion in a large salad bowl.

3. Just before serving pour on the dressing and toss well. Serve on individual salad plates with some of the cranberries and walnuts sprinkled on each portion.

Red Leaf Lettuce with Crumbled Goat Cheese and Honey-Mustard Dressing

The array of flavors in this tantalizing salad is a study of harmonious contrasts—sweet, pungent dressing, tangy goat cheese, salty olives, and spicy onion. It all comes together to delightfully whet the appetite for the next course.

Serves 4

Honey-Mustard Dressing

1 ½ tablespoons red wine vinegar

2 tablespoons honey

2 teaspoons Dijon-style mustard

2 tablespoons minced red onion

Dash salt

5 tablespoons mild olive oil

The Salad

4 cups bite-size pieces red leaf lettuce, washed and spun dry

4 cups bite-size pieces Romaine lettuce

⅔ cup slivered red onion

12 black olives, Niçoise, Kalamata, or other favorites

4 tablespoons crumbled soft mild goat cheese

1. To make the dressing, combine the vinegar and honey in a small bowl or jar and whisk to blend. This will take a minute or so. Whisk in all of the remaining dressing ingredients and set aside. If you are using a jar with a tight-fitting lid, add the remaining dressing ingredients and shake vigorously.

2. Combine the two lettuces and onion in a large salad bowl. Spoon on most of the dressing and toss well. Check to see if you need more dressing. Serve the salad on 4 salad plates. Place three olives on each portion, then place 1 tablespoon of crumbled goat cheese on each portion as well. Serve immediately.

Orange, Red Onion, and Black Olive Salad

This spectacular winter salad has become popular in recent years with good reason. The contrasting flavors and brilliant colors make it a perfect antidote to the winter blahs. Mediterranean in origin, it goes especially well with meals from that region, including most pasta dishes. Choose the sweetest and juiciest seedless oranges you can get. In New England that means navel oranges available in February, March, and April.

Serves 4

The Dressing
2 tablespoons red wine vinegar
1 small garlic clove, put through a press or minced
$^1/_4$ teaspoon salt
5 tablespoons olive oil

The Salad
4 large navel oranges, peeled
4 paper-thin slices red onion
16 oil-cured black olives, Niçoise olives, or other favorite olives

1. To make the dressing, combine its ingredients in a jar with a tight-fitting lid and shake vigorously.
2. To make the salad, slice the oranges crosswise into about 6 slices per orange. Arrange the slices by overlapping them around the rims of four plates. Separate the onion slices into rings and scatter them on top of the oranges. Place 4 olives on each plate. Drizzle some dressing over each portion. Let sit 30 minutes before serving.

Summer Tomato Salad

Perfectly ripe, juicy tomatoes are spotlighted in this seasonal salad, which is a delightful change of pace from more common salads based on leafy greens. Be certain to use only tomatoes that are at their prime; second-rate tomatoes just won't carry the dish.

Serves 4

The Dressing

¹/₄ cup olive oil

1 tablespoon balsamic vinegar

1 large garlic clove, put through a press or minced

Salt

Generous seasoning freshly ground black pepper

The Salad

3 medium, perfectly ripe summer tomatoes, each cut into about 10 wedges

1 ¹/₂ cups torn arugula

²/₃ cup freshly cooked or canned small white beans, well rinsed if canned

²/₃ cup slivered red onion

1. To make the dressing, combine the olive oil, vinegar, garlic, salt to taste, and pepper in a jar with a tight-fitting lid and shake vigorously.

2. Combine the salad ingredients in a large bowl. Just before serving pour on the dressing and toss gently. Serve on salad plates.

Mushroom Salad with Sun-Dried Tomato Vinaigrette

Thinly sliced mushrooms soak up a rosy-hued, garlicky dressing which makes them succulent and tender. Just wipe the mushrooms clean with paper towel; washing them will add too much moisture to these fabulous fungi.

Serves 4

The Dressing
3 loose sun-dried tomatoes (see Note)
1 large garlic clove, finely chopped
$\frac{1}{3}$ cup olive oil
3 tablespoons red wine vinegar
$\frac{1}{4}$ teaspoon salt
Generous seasoning freshly ground black pepper

1 pound very fresh white button mushrooms, wiped clean and thinly sliced
$\frac{1}{4}$ cup finely chopped flat-leaf parsley
Lettuce leaves

1. Place the sun-dried tomatoes in a small bowl and cover them with boiling water. Let soak 30 minutes. Drain the tomatoes and pat dry with paper towel. Cut the tomatoes into pieces, and put them in a blender along with the remaining dressing ingredients. Blend until smooth.

2. Place the mushrooms in a large bowl. Pour on the dressing and toss to coat well. Marinate the mushrooms for at least 4 hours or up to 24 hours. Cover and refrigerate if longer than 4 hours. Bring to room temperature before serving.

3. Just before serving mix the parsley into the mushrooms. Place some lettuce leaves on 4 salad plates. Serve a mound of mushrooms on each plate.

Note: If your sun-dried tomatoes are packed in oil, omit soaking them.

Spinach Salad with Sesame Dressing

Though it has an Asian accent, this salad goes well with many European-style entrees.

Serves 4

1 tablespoon sesame seeds

Sesame Dressing
1 ½ tablespoons red wine vinegar
1 small garlic clove, minced
½ teaspoon tamari soy sauce
Freshly ground black pepper
1 tablespoon oriental sesame oil
5 tablespoons canola oil

The Salad
8 cups well-washed spinach leaves, torn into small pieces, preferably from 1 large bunch
    flat-leaf spinach
2 scallions, very thinly sliced
4 large mushrooms, very thinly sliced
½ yellow or orange bell pepper, cut into thin slivers

1. Place a small bowl near the stove. Place the sesame seeds in a small saucepan and heat them over medium heat, swirling them around the pan continuously until they begin to get fragrant and just start to smoke. Don't take your eyes off them for one second! Immediately drop them into the bowl and let them cool.

2. To make the dressing, combine all the dressing ingredients in a jar with a tight-fitting lid and shake vigorously.

3. Combine the salad ingredients in a large salad bowl. Pour on the dressing and toss. Place a portion of salad on each salad plate, artfully arranging some pieces of pepper and mushroom on top. Sprinkle some sesame seeds on each portion.

Spinach Salad with Oranges and Toasted Pecans

Bursts of sweet, juicy oranges contrast splendidly with the slightly spicy dressing to make this salad a real charmer. If possible, purchase young delicate spinach in a bunch rather than thicker-leafed spinach packaged in a bag.

Serves 4

Creamy Orange-Cumin Dressing

1 tablespoon mayonnaise

1 tablespoon plain low-fat yogurt

2 teaspoons frozen orange juice concentrate

3 tablespoons olive oil

1 tablespoon red wine vinegar

1 small garlic clove, put through a press or minced

$1/4$ teaspoon ground cumin

Salt

Freshly ground black pepper to taste

The Salad

8 cups torn tender spinach leaves, well washed and spun dry

1 navel orange, peeled and separated into sections, then each section cut in half

4 thin slices red onion, separated into rings

20 pecan halves, toasted

1. To make the dressing, place the mayonnaise in a small bowl and beat it with a fork (this prevents any lumps from forming when the other ingredients are beaten in). Beat in the yogurt and orange juice concentrate, then briskly stir in the remaining dressing ingredients. Cover and chill the dressing for at least an hour for the flavors to develop.

2. Place the spinach on 4 salad plates. Drizzle one quarter of the dressing over each spinach portion. Top with the orange sections, onion rings, and pecans. Serve immediately.

Weekly Batch of Salad Dressing

I love having some vinaigrette in the refrigerator to fall back on when I want to quickly throw together a salad. I can modify a portion of it with some herbs or sesame oil to vary its original flavor, or just keep it as is—which is a delicious "all-purpose" dressing with garlic and lemon overtones. If you are pressed for time during the week, make a batch of this on the weekend and it will keep 7–10 days. You can use it on green salads, as well as marinated pasta salads, or cold bean or grain concoctions.

Makes 1 ¼ cups

3 tablespoons lemon juice

2 tablespoons red wine vinegar

2 garlic cloves, put through a press

2 teaspoons tamari soy sauce

¼ teaspoon salt

Generous seasoning freshly ground black pepper

1 cup olive oil

1. Combine all the ingredients in a jar with a tight-fitting lid and shake vigorously. Store in the refrigerator, but remove it at least 30 minutes before using it because the olive oil will solidify and, therefore, need to melt at room temperature.

Main-Course Salads

Summertime brings many seasonal pleasures, including the profusion of glorious, locally grown vegetables and herbs that, in their perfection, remind us of what is lost when food travels too far and for too long a time. With the emergence of hot weather comes a change in my kitchen that I readily welcome, and that is the reliance on main-course salads for many of our meals. I do make these dishes throughout the year, but nowhere near as often as I do when the temperature rises both outdoors and indoors. These salads benefit from being made in advance, and that works well with my desire to cook early in the day when it's cooler, and have a one-dish meal ready in the evening when I'm hot and sluggish.

If you have family members or friends who are hesitant to include various grains in their diets, these salads are a clever way to introduce them to ingredients they might otherwise shun. Garlicky vinaigrettes bring these medleys to life, and almost guarantee their widespread appeal. To extend these main-course salads into mini feasts, include some excellent crusty bread, a cheese platter, and some olives, and you've got an impressive spread with little work involved.

See also: *Marinated Fried Tofu and Vegetable Salad with Mesclun (page 206)*
Bow-Tie Pasta and Fried Tofu Salad with Sesame Dressing (page 210)
Soba and Fried Tofu Salad with Shredded Spinach (page 208)

Couscous Salad with Dried Cranberries and Pecans

Tangy, crimson-colored dried cranberries and toasted pecans are a dynamic combination in this special salad. If you plan to make it more than 2 hours in advance, hold back on adding the cucumbers until serving time so they will retain their special crunch.

Serves 4 as a main course

1 cup shelled pecans

1 ½ cups couscous

1 cup dried cranberries

½ teaspoon turmeric

2 cups boiling water

1 cup thawed frozen peas

3 scallions, very thinly sliced

2 medium cucumbers, peeled, seeded, and diced

¼ cup shredded fresh basil

Lemon Dressing

Zest of 1 lemon

⅓ cup lemon juice

3 garlic cloves, minced

½ teaspoon salt

Freshly ground black pepper

⅓ cup olive oil

1. Toast the pecans in a shallow pan in a preheated 350-degree oven until very fragrant, about 7 minutes. Set aside to cool.

2. Place the couscous, cranberries, and turmeric in a large bowl. Pour in the boiling water, stir, then cover the bowl with a large plate or foil. Let sit for 10 minutes. Remove the cover, then fluff the couscous with a fork. Cover again and let sit 5 more minutes.

3. Stir in the pecans, peas, scallions, cucumbers, and basil.

4. Combine the dressing ingredients in a jar with a tight-fitting lid and shake vigorously. Pour onto the couscous mixture and stir to blend. Let the salad sit at least 1 hour before serving to allow the flavors to blend. If longer than 1 hour, cover and chill, but then bring the salad to room temperature before serving. (Don't forget—if you make the salad more than an hour before you intend to serve it, hold back on adding the cucumbers until serving time or thereabouts.)

Rice Salad with Roasted Red Peppers, Chickpeas, and Feta Cheese

This piquant Greek-style salad is jam-packed with vegetables and flavor. I oftentimes cook the rice the night before or early in the day if I know the weather is going to be hot, then all I have to do is assemble it later on with no further cooking needed.

Serves 4 as a main course

2 1/2–3 cups cold cooked converted white rice or other long-grain white rice (made from 1 cup rice boiled in 2 1/4 cups water)

1 (16-ounce) can chickpeas, rinsed well and drained

3/4 cup finely diced feta cheese

2/3 cup diced roasted red peppers, store-bought or freshly roasted (page 19)

1/2 cup chopped fresh parsley

1/4 cup chopped fresh dill, or 2 teaspoons dried

3 scallions, very thinly sliced

The Dressing

1/4 cup fresh lemon juice

2 garlic cloves, put through a press or minced

Generous seasoning freshly ground black pepper

Salt

1/4 cup olive oil

1. Combine the rice, chickpeas, feta cheese, peppers, parsley, dill, and scallions in a large bowl and toss well.

2. Combine all the dressing ingredients in a jar with a tight-fitting lid and shake vigorously. Pour the dressing on the rice mixture and mix thoroughly. Let sit at least 1 hour or up to 8 hours before serving. Serve at room temperature.

Curried Rice Salad

This delicious salad is easy to assemble, and the result is an eye-catching palette of yellows and greens which looks quite lovely as a summer entree when served on a contrasting plate. Brown rice is preferable to white rice here because its nutty flavor enhances all the other components of this favorite salad.

Serves 4 as a main course

2 ½–3 cups cold cooked long-grain brown rice (made from 1 cup rice boiled in 2 cups water)

½ cup raisins

1 red-skinned apple, cut into ½-inch dice

⅓ cup chopped dry roasted peanuts

1 cup thawed frozen peas

3 scallions, thinly sliced

10 snow peas, cut in half diagonally

The Dressing

3 tablespoons fresh lemon juice

2 teaspoons minced gingerroot

2 garlic cloves, minced

2 teaspoons curry powder

½ teaspoon salt

Generous seasoning freshly ground pepper

¼ cup olive oil

1. Combine the rice, raisins, apple, peanuts, peas, scallions, and snow peas in a large bowl and toss well.

2. Combine all the dressing ingredients in a jar with a tight-fitting lid and shake vigorously. Pour the dressing on the salad and toss to coat well. Chill at least 1 hour or up to 8 hours, then bring to room temperature before serving.

Triple Rice Salad
with Dried Fruits and Nuts

Second to wheat in worldwide importance, rice has been the mainstay of the diet of millions of people across many cultures. I love to turn it into a main course, and the use of three types of rice here provides the full impact of this delicious, versatile grain. Chock full of color and texture, this salad is the perfect choice when you crave something wholesome yet light.

Serves 4 as a main course

3 cups water
$\frac{1}{4}$ teaspoon salt
1 teaspoon olive oil
$\frac{1}{2}$ cup wild rice, rinsed
$\frac{1}{2}$ cup long-grain brown rice, rinsed
$\frac{1}{2}$ cup converted or basmati white rice, rinsed
1 cup dried cranberries
$\frac{1}{3}$ cup currants
$\frac{1}{2}$ cup diced dried apricots (snip apricots with scissors into sixths)

The Dressing
$\frac{1}{4}$ cup fresh lemon juice
3 garlic cloves, minced
2 shallots, minced
$\frac{1}{2}$ teaspoon salt
Generous seasoning freshly ground black pepper
$\frac{1}{3}$ cup olive oil

$\frac{2}{3}$ cup whole pecans
3 scallions, very thinly sliced
$\frac{1}{2}$ cup chopped fresh parsley
2 tablespoons chopped fresh mint, or 2 teaspoons dried
1 tablespoon chopped fresh basil, or $\frac{1}{2}$ teaspoon dried

1. In a medium-size saucepan over high heat combine the water, salt, olive oil, wild rice, and brown rice. Cover the pan and bring to a boil. Reduce the heat to a simmer and cook 30 minutes.

2. Remove the cover and sprinkle in the white rice, being careful not to disturb the rice below. Cover the pan and cook about 20 minutes, or until all the water has been absorbed and the rice is just about to start sticking to the pot.

3. Meanwhile combine the dried cranberries, currants, and apricots in a large serving bowl. When the rice is cooked, carefully spoon it onto the dried fruit and toss just enough to incorporate it without making it gummy, a few strokes. Let the mixture cool completely. (The heat from the rice will plump up the dried fruit.)

4. Meanwhile make the dressing. Combine the lemon juice, garlic, shallots, salt, pepper, and olive oil in a jar with a tight-fitting lid and shake vigorously.

5. Gently stir the pecans, scallions, parsley, mint, and basil into the rice mixture. Pour on the dressing and toss. Chill and let marinate a few hours before serving. Serve at room temperature.

Asian Barley and Mushroom Salad

Barley's nubbiness is accentuated in this crunchy, yet light salad.

Serves 4 as a main course

1 cup barley, rinsed in a strainer
1 teaspoon plus 1 tablespoon canola oil
12 ounces thinly sliced mushrooms (4 ½ cups)

The Dressing
2 ½ tablespoons tamari soy sauce
1 ½ tablespoons oriental sesame oil
1 tablespoon Chinese rice wine or dry sherry
1 small garlic clove, minced

2 carrots, finely diced
2 scallions, very thinly sliced
Salt
Freshly ground black pepper

1. Fill a stockpot half full with water and bring it to a boil. Drop in the barley and 1 teaspoon of the canola oil. Reduce the heat to a lively simmer and cook 40 minutes.

2. Meanwhile heat the remaining tablespoon of canola oil in a large skillet over medium-high heat. Add the mushrooms and sauté until they are brown and their juices are rendered, then evaporated, about 10 minutes. Set aside to cool.

3. Drain the barley in a colander or large strainer. Place the barley in a large bowl.

4. Make the dressing by combining the soy sauce, sesame oil, rice wine, and garlic. Pour *half* the dressing on the barley and toss. Let the barley cool to room temperature.

5. Stir the mushrooms, carrots, and scallions into the barley along with the remaining dressing. Season with salt and pepper and toss well. Let marinate at least 1 hour before serving, or cover and chill up to 24 hours. Bring to room temperature before serving.

Chickpea Salad with Fennel, Tomatoes, and Olives

This is an ideal dish for a hot summer day because you can assemble it with no cooking at all. To complete the Mediterranean theme, serve this savory salad with French bread and goat cheese for a fabulous combination.

Serves 2–3 as a main course

The Dressing
1 tablespoon red wine vinegar
1 garlic clove, minced
½ teaspoon Dijon-style mustard
Salt
Generous seasoning freshly ground black pepper
3 tablespoons fruity olive oil

2 cups freshly cooked or canned chickpeas, rinsed thoroughly if canned
1 small fennel bulb, halved vertically and thinly sliced (1 ½ cups sliced); reserve feathery sprigs for garnish
2 ripe tomatoes, diced
10 black olives (your favorite kind), pitted and halved (see sidebar, opposite page)
½ cup thinly sliced red onion
⅓ cup chopped fresh parsley
2 tablespoons chopped fennel sprigs for garnish (see above)

1. To make the dressing, combine the vinegar, garlic, mustard, salt, and pepper in a large serving bowl and whisk to blend. Slowly whisk in the olive oil.

2. Stir in all the remaining ingredients except the fennel sprigs. Let the salad marinate at least 1 hour or up to 4 hours before serving. Garnish with fennel when ready to serve.

Olives

There are so many olives available that one can become dizzy from the choices. It seems pointless to list all the different varieties of olives because most stores don't label their olives with specific names.

When it comes to olives, you must find ones that suit your palate. What is wonderfully pungent to one person can be overwhelmingly caustic to another. I have found a fabulous black olive (sold locally) that I believe has been cured in brine but packed in a fruity, herb-laced olive oil. I can't get any information on these olives except from the huge can they are shipped in, which states only, "Greek Olives Packed in Oil." They are juicy, sweet, and meaty. To my taste, all other olives pale in comparison.

The best approach is to sample as many olives as you can, and stick to your favorites. If an olive is too dry, or salty, or pungent when you nibble on it, then chances are you won't enjoy it in a recipe.

Pitting Olives

It is not at all difficult to pit olives if you do it the following way: Put 1 olive on a heavy cutting board or other steady surface. Place the flat side of a large knife on the olive, then with your fist, thump the flat surface of the knife (the way you would remove the skin off garlic). This will loosen the pit, and now you can split the olive open with your fingers and remove the pit. Repeat this with the remaining olives, and you can count the pits to help you keep track of the number of olives you have prepared.

Tabbouli with Feta and Cucumbers

Bolstering traditional bulghur wheat salad with feta cheese and cucumber makes it into a substantial main-course salad teeming with flavor, color, and texture. There might appear to be an inordinate amount of parsley in this interpretation, but actually, classic tabbouli is a parsley salad with a little bulghur added, not the other way around.

Serves 4 as a main course

1 ½ cups golden bulghur wheat (preferably coarse-cut), rinsed in a strainer

½ cucumber, peeled, seeded, and finely diced

2 scallions, very thinly sliced

1 ½ cups very finely chopped fresh parsley

1 ½ tablespoons minced fresh mint

¾ cup (4 ounces) finely diced feta cheese

The Dressing

¼ cup fresh lemon juice

⅓ cup olive oil

½ teaspoon salt

Generous seasoning freshly ground black pepper

1. Place the bulghur in a medium-size bowl. Pour enough boiling water over it to cover by about 1 inch. Cover the bowl with a plate and let the bulghur sit for 30 minutes. In batches, scoop up some bulghur into a strainer, then press out all of its liquid with the back of a large spoon. Dump this bulghur into a large bowl. Repeat with the remaining bulghur. (Alternatively, you can place batches of bulghur in a cotton kitchen towel, twist the towel into a ball, then squeeze out all the liquid.) Let the bulghur cool completely.

2. Stir the vegetables, herbs, and feta cheese into the bulghur.

3. Whisk the lemon juice, olive oil, salt, and pepper together in a medium-size bowl. Pour onto the tabbouli and toss to coat. Chill at least 1 hour or up to 8 hours before serving. Serve cool, not cold.

Mediterranean White Bean Salad

The sun-drenched flavors of tomatoes, yellow peppers, and arugula dazzle when this salad is made during the peak of summer with homegrown or local produce. If you are using canned beans, choose a small, firm, white variety such as Great Northern or navy beans because canned cannellini (white kidney beans) are too soft for this salad. Crusty Tuscan-style bread is the ideal accompaniment.

Serves 4 as a main course

4 cups freshly cooked or canned small white beans (such as navy or Great Northern), rinsed and well drained if canned (2 [16-ounce] cans)
2 perfectly ripe tomatoes, cored and finely diced
½ cup slivered red onion
1 yellow bell pepper, cut into thin 2-inch-long strips

The Dressing
¼ cup olive oil
2 tablespoons lemon juice
1 large garlic clove, put through a press or minced
¼ teaspoon salt
Generous seasoning freshly ground black pepper

2 cups torn-up pieces arugula

1. Place the beans, tomatoes, onion, and pepper in a large bowl.
2. Combine the dressing ingredients in a jar with a tight-fitting lid and shake vigorously. Pour the dressing on the salad and toss well. Let sit 1–4 hours to marinate.
3. Just before serving, add the arugula and toss to thoroughly coat with the dressing. Serve immediately.

Lentil and Arugula Salad
with Feta Cheese

The slightly sweet tone of the balsamic dressing is a pleasing counterpoint to the peppery arugula and tangy feta cheese. This salad is wonderful as an entree with some crusty bread, or as a first course for a soup-centered meal.

Serves 4 as a main course

1 cup lentils

Balsamic Dressing
2 tablespoons balsamic vinegar
1 teaspoon Dijon-style mustard
1 large garlic clove, put through a press or minced
$\frac{1}{4}$ teaspoon salt
Generous seasoning freshly ground black pepper
$\frac{1}{4}$ cup olive oil

1 cup (5 ounces) finely cubed feta cheese
$\frac{1}{2}$ cup slivered red onion
1 cucumber, peeled, cut lengthwise and seeded, and cut into small dice
2 cups bite-size pieces arugula

1. Fill a medium-size saucepan with water and bring to a boil. Drop in the lentils and return the water to a boil, stirring occasionally. Reduce the heat a bit and cook the lentils about 20 minutes, or until tender but still slightly crunchy. Taste a few to be certain because you don't want mushy lentils.

2. Meanwhile combine the dressing ingredients in a jar with a tight-fitting lid and shake vigorously.

3. Drain the lentils in a colander and shake it a few times to remove all the liquid. Scrape the lentils into a large serving bowl, then pour on *half* the dressing. Toss to coat well.

Let the lentils cool to room temperature. (The lentils may be prepared to this point up to 8 hours in advance, covered, and chilled. Bring to room temperature before proceeding with the next step.)

4. Mix in the feta, onion, cucumber, arugula, and remaining dressing. Let sit at least 10 minutes but no more than 30 minutes before serving.

Soba Salad with Spicy Peanut Sauce

This spicy sauce has sweet overtones that go well with the nutty flavor of soba.

Serves 3–4 as a main course

1 pound soba (buckwheat spaghetti)

Peanut Sauce
¹⁄₃ cup natural-style peanut butter
¹⁄₄ cup tamari soy sauce
1 ¹⁄₂ tablespoons pale dry sherry
3 tablespoons brown sugar
2 ¹⁄₂ tablespoons oriental sesame oil
1 tablespoon water
2 teaspoons minced gingerroot
A few dashes cayenne

1 carrot, very finely chopped
2 scallions, very thinly sliced

1. Bring a large stockpot of water to a boil for the soba.
2. Meanwhile make the sauce. Combine the peanut butter and soy sauce in a medium-size bowl, and, using a fork, beat them together until smooth. Beat in all the remaining sauce ingredients.
3. Cook the soba until al dente, about 5 minutes. Taste a strand at about 4 minutes so you don't overcook it. It should still be chewy when done. You have to be careful not to over-cook soba because the noodles will break into small pieces when you toss them with the sauce; on the other hand, you don't want them hard. Drain in a colander, then rinse the soba under cold running water. Drain again thoroughly.
4. Place the soba in a large serving bowl. Spoon on the sauce and toss thoroughly. Sprinkle the carrot and scallions over the top and serve.

Summer Spaghetti Salad

At the peak of summer when tomatoes and basil boast their glory by dazzling us with their splendid perfumes, that is the time to make this classic marinated salad. I like to start this early in the day so the flavors get a chance to meld.

Serves 4 as a main course

The Dressing
2 tablespoons red wine vinegar
3 large garlic cloves, minced
$\frac{1}{2}$ teaspoon salt
Generous seasoning freshly ground black pepper
$\frac{1}{3}$ cup olive oil

1 pound spaghetti
3 medium ripe tomatoes, cored, seeded, and finely diced
1 cup finely shredded fresh basil
1 cup chopped arugula *or* chopped fresh parsley
$\frac{1}{4}$ cup toasted pine nuts

1. Bring a large stockpot of water to a boil.
2. Meanwhile combine the ingredients for the dressing in a jar with a tight-fitting lid and shake vigorously.
3. Drop the spaghetti into the boiling water and cook until al dente. Taste a strand to avoid overcooking. Drain very well in a colander, then place the spaghetti in a very large serving bowl. Pour on *half* the dressing and toss to thoroughly coat the strands. Let cool to room temperature, tossing occasionally.
4. Mix in the tomatoes, basil, arugula, pine nuts, and the remaining dressing and let marinate at least one hour or up to 8 hours before serving. If you chill the salad, bring it to room temperature before serving, then taste to see if it needs more salt.

Thai Noodle and Green Bean Salad

Mint, basil, and cilantro come together to create an enchanting backdrop to this sesame-flavored dish. I love all Asian-style noodles, but this is among my favorites for its intriguing blend of flavors.

Serves 4 as a main course

1 pound spaghetti

The Marinade

3 tablespoons peanut or canola oil

3 tablespoons oriental sesame oil

3 tablespoons lime juice

3 tablespoons tamari soy sauce

2 tablespoons brown sugar

3 garlic cloves, minced

2 teaspoons minced gingerroot

$\frac{1}{2}$ teaspoon crushed red pepper flakes

$\frac{1}{2}$ teaspoon salt

1 pound green beans, each cut in half

3 scallions, very thinly sliced

2 tablespoons finely shredded fresh basil

2 tablespoons finely chopped fresh mint

1 tablespoon finely chopped cilantro

1. Bring a large stockpot of water to a boil for the noodles. Meanwhile combine the marinade ingredients in a medium-size bowl and set aside.

2. Drop the green beans in the boiling water and cook just until tender yet still slightly crunchy, about 5 minutes. Taste one to test. Scoop out the green beans with a strainer or slotted spoon and place in a bowl filled with ice-cold water to stop any further cooking. Dump out the water and repeat until the green beans are cold throughout. (Taste one.)

Drain thoroughly and place the green beans in a large serving bowl. Stir in the scallions, basil, mint, and cilantro.

3. Drop the spaghetti into the boiling water and cook until al dente. Drain thoroughly in a colander, then rinse under cold water. Shake the colander vigorously to remove all excess water. Mix the spaghetti with the green bean mixture.

4. Pour the marinade on the noodles and toss gently with tongs. Tossing occasionally to coat it with sauce, let marinate at room temperature at least 2 hours or up to 24 hours before serving. (Cover and chill the noodles if longer than 4 hours, then bring to room temperature before serving.)

Mint

Mint has moseyed its way into my kitchen recently, mostly via Thai and Middle Eastern cooking, and I'm finding that it's an herb I now always want to have on hand. It lends such a cool, vibrant tone and harmonizes well with many other flavors. I grow spearmint in my garden, or rather this persistent, hardy herb grows itself. From the spring through the fall I can snip mint as I please.

But what about the winter? I have found a source for dried mint at my local health food store. It sells peppermint and spearmint in bulk, the latter almost always being my choice. In desperation I have even ripped open mint tea bags, and have, consequently, saved a recipe or two.

Add mint to the selection of herbs you cook with, and it won't be long before you find it indispensable to the dishes it enhances.

Ziti and Broccoli Salad
with Sun-Dried Tomato Pesto

This is a hearty pasta salad with a robust sauce—just the thing you want when your "salad" is the main event.

Serves 4-6

1 pound ziti

The Pesto
2 ounces (about 13) loose sun-dried tomatoes
$\frac{1}{3}$ cup olive oil
2 garlic cloves, finely chopped
2 tablespoons chopped fresh basil, or 1 teaspoon dried
$\frac{1}{2}$ cup chopped fresh parsley
3 tablespoons finely chopped walnuts
2 tablespoons grated Parmesan cheese
$\frac{1}{2}$ teaspoon salt
Generous seasoning freshly ground black pepper

4-5 cups tiny broccoli florets (from 1 bunch broccoli)

1. Bring a large stockpot of water to a boil for the pasta.
2. To make the pesto, steam the sun-dried tomatoes in a vegetable steamer until they are soft, about 7 minutes. Remove and let cool to room temperature.
3. In a food processor combine the sun-dried tomatoes, olive oil, and garlic and process until smooth. Add the basil and parsley and pulse a few times to finely chop. Scrape the pesto into a bowl, then stir in the walnuts, Parmesan cheese, salt, and pepper by hand.
4. When the water comes to a boil, drop in the broccoli. Cook 2-3 minutes, or until crisp yet tender. Scoop out with a strainer and immerse it in a bowl of cold water to stop any further cooking. Drain the broccoli, then drop it onto a cotton kitchen towel and pat dry. Place in a large serving bowl.

5. Cook the ziti until al dente. Before you drain it, remove 1 tablespoon of the pasta water and stir it into the pesto. Drain the ziti in a colander, then rinse under cold running water. Shake the colander vigorously to remove all the water. Mix the ziti together with the broccoli.

6. Scrape the pesto onto the pasta and broccoli. Toss thoroughly to evenly coat it. Serve immediately or chill and let marinate up to 48 hours. Serve at room temperature.

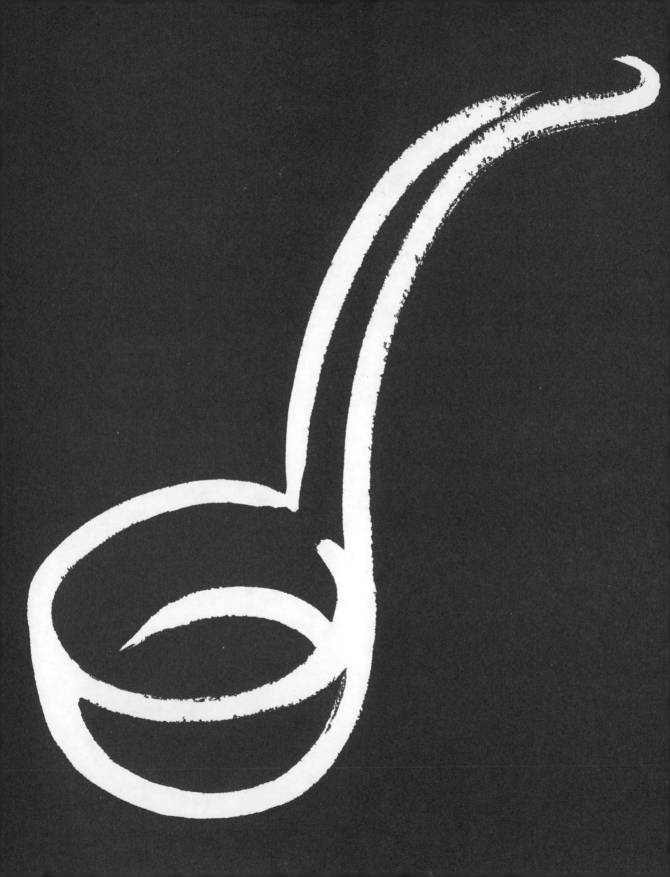

Substantial Soups

For the busy cook who wants to eat fresh, wholesome foods yet often finds herself in a last-minute crunch, few things in the kitchen can be more of a godsend than a pot of home-made soup in her refrigerator or freezer. Making soup is a task that all food lovers should embrace because it uses time at the stove so efficiently, while producing a one-pot meal that is nutritionally sound and restorative.

Furthermore, not many dishes we prepare actually benefit from sitting around a few days, but herein lies soup's greatest asset. If the busy cook can cultivate the habit of preparing a pot of soup when time allows, e.g., the weekend, then the reward for this advance thinking can be enjoyed throughout the week when time is in short supply. One can also easily multiply these benefits by doubling soup recipes and freezing a portion. It doesn't take twice the amount of time, perhaps only 10 extra minutes of chopping vegetables, yet the results of our efforts are significantly increased.

Because stock is the foundation of most soups and provides a layer of flavor upon which other flavors build, its value cannot be overestimated. This does not mean, however, that you must create your own stocks from scratch in order to have a delicious soup, but it does mean that you should search for a good-quality stock if you are going to use a store-bought product. (Read About Vegetable Stocks, page 11.)

So with a favorite soup stock in hand, a large pot, and a commitment to a bit of advance planning, let's make some soup!

Chickpea and Swiss Chard Soup with Parmesan Crostini

The building of layers of flavor in thick vegetable stews makes them especially inviting, but equally appealing to me are simple soups with just a few ingredients whose flavors are transported in a tasty broth. Although you can enjoy this soup just after you make it, it will benefit from being made a few hours in advance so the stock can really develop the garlicky undertones.

Serves 4 as a main course

$\frac{1}{4}$ cup olive oil

1 medium onion, very finely diced

8 garlic cloves, minced

$\frac{1}{4}$ teaspoon crushed red pepper flakes

8 cups vegetable stock, store-bought or homemade (page 13)

2 tablespoons tomato paste mixed with $\frac{1}{2}$ cup water

4 cups freshly cooked or canned chickpeas, well rinsed and drained if canned (2 [16-ounce] cans)

8 cups (about $\frac{3}{4}$ pound) finely shredded Swiss chard leaves

1 teaspoon salt

Parmesan Crostini

8 thin slices French bread

1 tablespoon olive oil

1 $\frac{1}{2}$ tablespoons grated Parmesan cheese

1. Heat the oil in a large stockpot over medium heat. Add the onion and cook, stirring often, for 3 minutes. Mix in the garlic and crushed pepper flakes and sauté 5 minutes, or until the onion is tender.

2. Add the stock, tomato paste mixture, and chickpeas and bring to a boil. Reduce the heat to a lively simmer and cook 10 minutes. Stir in the Swiss chard and salt and simmer 10 minutes.

3. Remove 2 cups of the soup and puree it in a blender or food processor. Return it to the pot.

4. To make the crostini, preheat the oven to 300 degrees. Using a pastry brush, lightly brush both sides of each French bread slice with some olive oil. Place them on a baking sheet and bake 5 minutes. Turn them over and bake 5 more minutes. Sprinkle the Parmesan cheese on top of each crostini, and return the crostini to the oven. Bake 5 minutes or until golden all over. Let cool completely before serving alongside the soup.

Mediterranean Vegetable Soup with Feta Cheese

As odd as it may sound, this soup's hauntingly good flavor is reminiscent of bouillabaisse, even though that soup is based on seafood. The interplay of fennel, tomato, and white wine creates a sensational broth that begs for crusty French bread to be dipped into it. Leftover fennel can be used another day in such recipes as Green Leaf Salad with Fennel, Apple, and Pecans (page 72), or Chickpea Salad with Fennel, Tomatoes, and Olives (page 94), or Leek, Fennel, and Goat Cheese Frittata (page 170).

Serves 4 as a main course

3 tablespoons olive oil

2 onions, very finely diced

6 garlic cloves, minced

¼ teaspoon crushed red pepper flakes

1 cup dry white wine

1 (16-ounce) can tomatoes, very finely chopped with their juice

6 cups vegetable stock, store-bought or homemade (page 13)

1½ cups thinly sliced fennel (from ½ medium bulb), reserve feathery sprigs

½ teaspoon dried oregano

½ teaspoon salt

Generous seasoning freshly ground black pepper

⅓ cup orzo (rice-shaped pasta)

½ cup chopped fresh parsley

½–¾ cup crumbled feta cheese

⅓ cup chopped fennel sprigs (see above)

1. Heat the oil in a large stockpot over medium heat. Add the onions, garlic, and red pepper flakes and sauté, stirring frequently, until the onions are tender, about 10 minutes.

2. Pour in the wine and boil until reduced by half. Stir in the tomatoes, stock, fennel, oregano, salt, and pepper and bring to a boil. Cook the soup 20 minutes, stirring occasionally.

3. Mix in the orzo and parsley and cook 10 minutes more. Serve the stew in bowls with about 1 tablespoon of feta cheese sprinkled on top of each serving, then top with some chopped fennel sprigs.

Don't Skip the Parsley

We are all guilty of allowing little bundles of fresh herbs to wilt and perish in our refrigerators because of neglect and forgetfulness. But this should never happen to parsley. It has such a fresh and compatible flavor that it can enhance almost anything, and so should disappear rather quickly.

Before the days when fresh herbs were readily available in the United States, dried parsley was used as a garnish and flavor was not an expectation. One could easily omit the parsley and the dish wouldn't suffer. This has all changed with the availability of fresh herbs in the American kitchen. We can now appreciate parsley as the ancient Greeks did, who prized it for medicinal purposes; the Romans enjoyed it as a culinary herb.

The vivid, harmonious flavor of fresh parsley enhances any dish in which it's included. Parsley doesn't usually define the character of a dish the way basil or other assertive herbs can; however, it accents the surrounding flavors with a welcome piquancy while providing a tone of freshness.

I purchase or grow flat-leaf Italian parsley rather than the curly-leaf variety because I prefer its appearance and find that it chops into more attractive pieces. I doubt that one could discern a difference in flavor between the two, although many cooks claim they can. Parsley is one green that I wash before storing in the refrigerator; that way it is readily available to use in soups, salads, sandwich spreads, and sauces. It will store better than most greens and herbs if it is spun dry in a salad spinner, then stored in a plastic bag with a paper towel placed at the bottom of the bag to absorb any excess moisture.

So don't skip the parsley; it adds a delicious supporting flavor to your dish.

Kale, Butternut Squash, and White Bean Soup

Three highly nutritious foods come together in this soup, lending it vibrant color and flavor. For a fitting accompaniment, try Crostini (page 16) spread with goat cheese.

Serves 4–6 as a main course

⅓ cup olive oil

2 large onions, diced

10 cups vegetable stock, store-bought or homemade (page 13)

1 cup finely diced canned tomatoes, with their liquid

2 teaspoons finely chopped fresh rosemary, or ½ teaspoon dried

½ teaspoon salt

Generous seasoning freshly ground black pepper

1 tiny butternut squash (1 pound), peeled, seeded, and diced (2 cups diced)

2 cups freshly cooked or canned small white beans, well rinsed if canned

½ pound kale (weight with stems), ripped off its stems and leaves cut into shreds (chiffonade) (4 cups shredded leaves)

Grated Parmesan cheese (optional)

1. Heat the oil in a large stockpot over medium heat. Add the onions and sauté until tender, about 10 minutes.

2. Stir in the stock, tomatoes, rosemary, salt, and pepper and bring to a boil. Add the squash and reduce the heat to a lively simmer. Cook 30 minutes, or until the squash is tender.

3. Add the beans and kale and cook 15 more minutes. Serve with grated Parmesan cheese, if desired.

Split Pea and Barley Soup

My neighbor, Clare Ward, gave me the idea of adding barley to split pea soup and it has proven to be just one more demonstration of her finely tuned palate. The creamy backdrop of pea soup is delightful with the nubbiness of barley. This soup has become a cold-weather favorite in our house, its appeal further enhanced by the fact that I always seem to have these ingredients on hand.

Serves 4

14 cups water
1 pound green split peas
½ cup barley, rinsed in a strainer
1 tablespoon olive oil
1 bay leaf
2 tablespoons unsalted butter
2 medium onions, diced
4 garlic cloves, minced
2 carrots, finely diced
1 celery rib, finely diced
1 teaspoon fresh thyme, or ½ teaspoon dried
1 teaspoon salt
Freshly ground black pepper to taste

1. In a large stockpot combine the water, split peas, barley, olive oil, and bay leaf. Bring to a boil, stirring occasionally, then reduce the heat to a lively simmer. Cook the soup, continuing to stir periodically, for 30 minutes.
2. Meanwhile melt the butter in a medium-size skillet over medium heat. Add the onions and garlic and sauté until the onions are golden brown, about 10 minutes.

3. Stir the onions into the soup along with the carrots, celery, thyme, salt, and pepper. Cook, now stirring frequently to prevent the soup from sticking as it thickens, for 30 more minutes. The soup is ready when the peas have almost totally dissolved and the barley and vegetables are tender. The soup will thicken as it cools in the serving bowls, so thin it with more water if necessary so that its consistency resembles heavy cream. Remove and discard the bay leaf before serving the soup.

Creamy White Bean Soup
with Red Pepper Swirl

This luscious soup has a rich, silken texture. The red pepper swirl is achieved by spooning a small amount of red pepper puree on the center of each portion and using a knife to swirl it around.

I prefer to use a blender rather than a food processor for both the red peppers and the soup because it produces a perfectly smooth texture—just what you want for this graceful soup.

Serves 4 as a main course

3 tablespoons fruity olive oil

2 large onions, diced

2 celery ribs, thinly sliced*

6 garlic cloves, minced

6 cups vegetable stock, store-bought or homemade (page 13)

6 cups freshly cooked or canned cannellini (white kidney beans), rinsed well in a strainer if canned (3 [15-ounce] cans)

1 tablespoon red wine vinegar

$\frac{1}{2}$ teaspoon chopped fresh rosemary, or $\frac{1}{4}$ teaspoon dried, crumbled

$\frac{1}{2}$ teaspoon salt

Generous seasoning freshly ground black pepper

Red Pepper Puree

1 cup roasted red peppers, freshly roasted (page 19) or from 1 (7-ounce) jar, drained

1 garlic clove, minced

1. Heat the oil in a large stockpot over medium-high heat. Add the onions and celery and sauté until they begin to brown, about 10 minutes. Stir in the garlic and cook 5 minutes, stirring often. (The browning of these vegetables will flavor the soup, so keep the heat high enough to achieve that color.)

Celery is an essential flavor in this soup, so don't omit it.

2. Add the stock, beans, vinegar, rosemary, salt, and pepper. Bring the soup to a boil, then reduce the heat to a simmer. Cook 20 minutes, or until the celery is very soft.

3. Meanwhile make the red pepper puree by combining the red peppers and garlic in a blender and pureeing them. Scrape the mixture into a small bowl. Rinse out the blender container.

4. In batches puree the soup until it is perfectly smooth. You can pour the pureed batches into a smaller saucepan at this point. The thickness of the finished soup should be like heavy cream; thin with some stock if it is too thick.

5. To serve, ladle the soup into bowls. Spoon a generous mound of red pepper puree in the center. Using a knife, swirl the puree to make a lovely design, such as irregular radiating lines from the center.

Butternut Squash Soup

I created this delicious soup on an unforgiving day in March when it seemed as if spring would never come. It was a burst of sunshine in a bowl, bolstered by that savory trio of parsley, garlic, and Parmesan cheese. This is not a smooth soup, as are most versions with butternut squash, but rather cubes of squash with rice and a generous amount of parsley afloat in a delicious broth. The ginger only slightly accents the soup without dominating it, so be sure to include it.

Serves 4 as a main course

¼ cup olive oil

2 large onions, finely diced

6 garlic cloves, minced

1 teaspoon minced gingerroot

10 cups vegetable stock, store-bought or homemade (page 13)

6 cups (2½ pounds) diced butternut squash (½-inch dice)

½ cup white rice, preferably converted or basmati

1 teaspoon salt

Generous seasoning freshly ground black pepper

1 cup minced fresh parsley

Grated Parmesan cheese

1. Heat the oil in a large stockpot over medium heat. Add the onions, garlic, and gingerroot and sauté until the onions are golden, about 10 minutes.

2. Pour in the stock and bring it to a boil. Stir in the squash, rice, salt, and pepper and bring the soup again to a boil, stirring often. Reduce it to a simmer, then cook it about 45 minutes, or until the squash and rice are very tender.

3. Remove about 2 cups of the soup and puree it in a blender or processor. Return it to the soup pot. Taste to correct the seasoning. Just before serving, stir in the parsley. Serve in bowls with a generous spoonful of grated Parmesan sprinkled on top.

Kale and Potato Soup

Such a simple soup yet so satisfying and flavorful. Caldo verde, the classic Portuguese soup, is very similar to this version; however, I've omitted the common addition of sausage and mimicked its flavor with this light garlic broth, which wonderfully enhances the kale and potatoes without overpowering them.

When I've been overindulging because of a long stretch of company, or holiday festivities, or too many restaurant meals in a row, I inevitably turn to this soup for its restorative qualities. Kale simmered in broth tenderizes that leafy green—one of my all-time favorite vegetables—and brings out its best qualities.

Serves 3–4 as a main course

3 tablespoons olive oil

4 garlic cloves, minced

¼ teaspoon crushed red pepper flakes

8 cups vegetable stock, store-bought or homemade (page 13)

2 medium boiling (waxy) potatoes, peeled and finely diced (2 cups diced)

½ pound kale (weight with stems), leaves ripped off stems and finely shredded (about 7 cups shredded)

½ teaspoon salt

1. Heat the oil in a large stockpot over medium heat. Add the garlic and red pepper flakes and cook 1 minute. Do not let the garlic get at all brown. Pour in the stock, raise the heat to high, then bring to a boil.

2. Add the potatoes, lower the heat to a lively simmer, and cook 15 minutes. Stir in the kale and salt and cook the soup 15 more minutes.

Fresh Tomato Corn Soup

This is a splendid summer soup whose success is completely dependent upon juicy, ripe tomatoes at their peak and sweet ears of fresh corn. It will fill your house with an irresistible aroma, yet all it needs is about a half hour of cooking. Although it is not at all fussy to prepare this low-fat soup, you will need a food mill to puree and strain it. And don't hesitate to try this recipe if you've never cut corn off its cob; it couldn't be easier to do.

Serves 4 as a main course

2 tablespoons unsalted butter

2 large onions, chopped

4 garlic cloves, chopped

1 celery rib (preferably with leaves attached), chopped

1 carrot, finely chopped

1/2 cup chopped parsley

3 pounds (5 very large) ripe tomatoes, cored and chopped

4 cups Tomato-Scallion Stock (page 14), or vegetable stock, store-bought or homemade (page 13)

1/2 teaspoon sugar

1 teaspoon salt

Generous seasoning freshly ground black pepper

2 ears corn, shucked

Shredded basil for garnish

1. Melt the butter in a large stockpot over medium-high heat. Add the onions, garlic, celery, and carrot and sauté, tossing frequently, until the vegetables begin to get brown, about 10 minutes.

2. Stir in the parsley, tomatoes, stock, sugar, salt, and pepper. Bring the soup to a boil, then reduce the heat to a lively simmer, and cook the soup 20 minutes. Let the soup cool.

3. While the soup is cooling, cut the kernels off the cob by standing the cob on its wide end and slicing the kernels off from the tip of the cob to the bottom.

4. In batches put the soup through a food mill, then discard the solids that remain. Drop the corn in the soup, then return it to a boil. Cook 10 minutes, or until the corn is tender yet still slightly crunchy. Serve in bowls, with a few shreds of basil as a garnish.

Curried Red Lentil Soup
with Coconut Milk

Two of my other cookbooks have recipes for curried red lentil soup because I am so enamored of this delicious legume and its natural mating with curry. This version contains coconut milk and lime juice, which make it an even more spectacular soup. You'll love this triumphant blending of flavors.

Serves 4 as a main course

4 cups water
1 tablespoon vegetable oil
1 ½ cups red lentils, rinsed in a strainer
¾ teaspoon salt
4 cups very hot water
2 ½ cups unsweetened desiccated coconut (see Note)
1 tablespoon unsalted butter
1 onion, diced
4 garlic cloves, minced
1 teaspoon minced fresh gingerroot
1 teaspoon turmeric
1 teaspoon ground coriander
1 teaspoon ground cumin
Dash cayenne
Juice of 1 lime

1. Combine the water, oil, lentils, and salt in a 3-quart saucepan and bring to a boil, stirring occasionally. Reduce the heat to a simmer and cook 20 minutes, stirring often.

2. Meanwhile make the coconut milk by combining the hot water and coconut in a blender or food processor and blending it for 2 minutes. In batches, pour it through a strainer over a large bowl and press out as much milk as you can from the coconut by

using the back of a large spoon. Discard the coconut pulp. Mix the coconut milk into the lentil mixture and simmer 20 minutes, stirring frequently.

3. Melt the butter in a medium-size skillet over medium heat. Add the onion, garlic, and ginger and sauté until the onion is golden brown, about 10 minutes. Sprinkle in the spices and "toast" them 2 minutes. Scrape this mixture into the soup, then add the juice of the lime. Cook the soup 10 more minutes, stirring often. The soup is done when the lentils have dissolved. (If you make the soup in advance—a good idea to help develop the flavors—it will get thick when it cools. After reheating it over low heat, check the consistency. If it is too thick, thin it with a little water.)

Note: Unsweetened desiccated coconut can be purchased at natural foods stores and some specialty shops. It will last up to a year in the refrigerator.

Leek and Potato Chowder

In the fall and winter when the price of leeks goes down, I am eager to make this simple yet delicious chowder because it so splendidly spotlights the incomparable sweet flavor of leeks, one of my favorite vegetables. This recipe doubles or triples easily, so don't hesitate to make it for a crowd, if the occasion arises.

Serves 3 as a main course

3 large leeks
2 tablespoons unsalted butter
3 cups light vegetable stock, store-bought or homemade (page 13)
3 medium-large boiling (waxy) potatoes, peeled and finely cubed
1 teaspoon salt
Generous seasoning freshly ground black pepper
1 ¹/₄ cups milk
¹/₄ cup sour cream
Minced parsley or chives for garnish

1. To clean the leeks, cut off and discard their root ends plus all the dark green leaves except for 2 inches closest to the white part. Cut the leeks in half lengthwise, then rinse them thoroughly under cold running water, flipping through the leaves to rid them of *all* sand. Thinly slice the leeks.

2. Heat the butter in a large stockpot over medium heat. Sauté the leeks until tender, about 10 minutes. Do not let them get brown. Add the stock, potatoes, salt, and pepper and bring to a boil. Partially cover the pot and cook the soup about 20 minutes, or until the potatoes are tender.

3. Puree about two thirds of the soup in a food processor or blender and return it to the pot. Stir in the milk and sour cream. Reheat until hot, but do not let the soup boil. Serve in bowls with parsley or chives sprinkled on top.

Mixed Mushroom and Barley Soup

Mushroom lovers take note—a mixture of exotic and common mushrooms creates a tantalizing broth that becomes a veritable balm on a frosty evening. Do try to make this soup in advance—at least 6 hours or preferably 1–2 days—because the mushroom flavor will be intensified, and that can only mean more of a good thing.

Serves 4 as a main course

3 tablespoons olive oil

2 medium onions, finely diced

4 garlic cloves, minced

½ pound common white button mushrooms, coarsely chopped into almond-size pieces

½ pound exotic mushrooms, such as shiitake, portobello, and oyster mushrooms, coarsely chopped into almond-size pieces

10 cups Mushroom Stock (page 15) or vegetable stock, either store-bought or homemade (page 13)

½ cup barley, rinsed in a strainer

2 carrots, finely chopped

2 tablespoons tamari soy sauce

2 tablespoons dry sherry

1 teaspoon fresh thyme, or ½ teaspoon dried

½ teaspoon salt

Generous seasoning freshly ground pepper

1. In a large stockpot heat the oil over medium-high heat. Add the onions and garlic and sauté until the onions turn golden brown, at least 10 minutes.

2. Stir in the mushrooms and sauté until they become brown, about 10 minutes. Stir often and scrape the bottom of the pot to loosen those tasty bits that adhere to the pot.

3. Mix in all the remaining ingredients and bring to a boil. Lower the heat to a lively simmer, cover the pan, and cook 45–60 minutes, or until the barley is tender. If the soup is too thick, thin with a little stock.

Peanut Soup

Here's a delicious African-inspired, non-dairy soup with a lot of flavor. I prefer to puree it in a food processor rather than in a blender because the processor allows the peanut butter to retain a little texture.

Serves 4–6

2 tablespoons canola oil

6 garlic cloves, minced

3 medium onions, finely diced

2 celery ribs, thinly sliced

3 carrots, finely diced

A few dashes cayenne pepper (or more to taste)

6 cups vegetable stock, store-bought or homemade (page 13)

1/2 teaspoon salt

Generous seasoning freshly ground pepper

1 cup plus 2 tablespoons natural-style peanut butter

1 1/2 teaspoons tamari soy sauce

Juice of 1 lemon

1 1/2 teaspoons brown sugar

Minced cilantro or fresh parsley for garnish

1. Heat the oil in a large stockpot over medium heat. Add the garlic and onions and sauté until the onions begin to soften, about 5 minutes. Add the celery and carrots and sauté, stirring often, until the vegetables begin to brown, about 10 minutes.

2. Stir in the cayenne, stock, salt, and pepper and bring to a boil. Lower the heat and simmer 10 minutes. Whisk in the peanut butter, then remove the soup from the heat.

3. In batches, puree the soup in a food processor until somewhat smooth, but with a little texture remaining. Return it to the pot. Stir in the soy sauce, lemon juice, and brown sugar. Serve in bowls with a little cilantro or parsley as a garnish.

Sweet Potato and Peanut Soup

The peanuts are barely discernible in this savory soup, yet provide an important layer of flavoring. Both fresh ginger and ground ginger bolster it all to make this a tonic on a chilly fall or winter night.

Serves 4 as a main course

2 tablespoons olive oil

4 garlic cloves, minced

1 tablespoon minced gingerroot

3 large onions, diced

2 tablespoons dry-roasted unsalted peanuts, plus finely chopped peanuts for garnish

½ teaspoon ground (powdered) ginger

6 cups vegetable stock (plus extra for thinning), store-bought or homemade (page 13)

3 large yams or sweet potatoes (2 ½ pounds), peeled and cut into ½-inch dice

1 tablespoon brown sugar

Pinch cinnamon

1 teaspoon salt

Generous seasoning freshly ground black pepper

1 tablespoon unsalted butter

1. In a large stockpot heat the oil over medium-high heat. Add the garlic, gingerroot, onions, and peanuts and sauté, stirring often, until the onions begin to brown, at least 10 minutes. Sprinkle on the ground ginger, toss, and cook 1 minute.

2. Stir in the stock, yams, brown sugar, cinnamon, salt, and pepper. Partially cover the pot, and cook the soup until the yams are soft, about 20 minutes.

3. Let the soup cool slightly, then remove about 2 cups of it and set that portion aside. Puree the soup in a few batches and return it to the pot. Stir in the reserved soup and the butter. Reheat the soup and check its consistency; it should be like heavy cream. Serve in bowls and garnish with some chopped peanuts.

Spinach Soup with Couscous and Lemon

The tender, fluffy texture of couscous lends a delicate touch to this tasty soup. If possible, make it early in the day so the flavors have a chance to develop.

Serves 4–6 as a main course

2 tablespoons olive oil

4 garlic cloves, minced

2 shallots, finely diced

10 cups vegetable stock, store-bought or homemade (page 13)

½ cup couscous

2 cups freshly cooked or canned chickpeas, rinsed thoroughly and well drained if canned

1 (1-pound) bunch or 1 (10-ounce) package fresh spinach, washed, stems discarded, and leaves torn into small pieces, about 10 cups

1 cup chopped fresh parsley

6 scallions, very thinly sliced

1 tablespoon chopped fresh dill, or 1 teaspoon dried

1 teaspoon salt

Generous seasoning freshly ground black pepper

Juice of 1 lemon

1 tablespoon unsalted butter

1. Heat the oil in a large stockpot over medium heat. Add the garlic and shallots and cook 2 minutes, stirring often. Pour in the stock and bring it to a boil.

2. Stir in the couscous and chickpeas and cook at medium heat for 10 minutes, stirring often. Add the spinach, parsley, *half* the scallions, the dill, salt, and pepper. Cook the soup 10 more minutes, stirring frequently. (The soup can be prepared to this point up to 2 days in advance.)

3. Just before serving stir in the lemon juice, butter, and remaining scallions.

Black Bean Chili

This gutsy chili, which is so easy to prepare, could be the perfect antidote to a chilly (no pun intended) evening. Hot buttered corn bread could only make things better.

Serves 6

2 tablespoons olive oil

6 garlic cloves, minced

2 onions, very finely diced

$^1/_4$ teaspoon crushed red pepper flakes

1 tablespoon chili powder

1 tablespoon ground cumin

1 teaspoon dried oregano

1 bay leaf

1 (28-ounce) can imported plum tomatoes, finely chopped with their juice

1 tablespoon tamari soy sauce

3 cups water

3 tablespoons tomato paste

$^3/_4$ teaspoon salt

8 cups freshly cooked ($1^1/_2$ pounds dry) or 4 (15-ounce) cans black beans, rinsed and well drained if canned

1 tablespoon red wine vinegar

Minced parsley for garnish

1. Heat the oil in a large stockpot over medium heat. Add the garlic, onions, and red pepper flakes and cook 1 minute. Stir in the chili powder and cumin and cook 2 minutes, stirring often.

2. Stir in all the remaining ingredients except the parsley and bring to a boil. Reduce the heat to a lively simmer and cook about 30 minutes, or until the chili is thick but not pasty. Remove the bay leaf. Serve in bowls and garnish with the parsley.

Sweet Potato Chili

I'm sure many Tex-Mex aficionados are appalled by the liberties cooks have taken with chili in recent years, but I find the temptation to experiment with new versions hard to resist. Here, sweet potatoes provide a lively contrast in flavor to the spicy backdrop of chili, and together with the vegetables and beans create a dazzling palette of color. Because the sweet potatoes take the place of a portion of beans that would normally be in this amount of chili, you'll find this version lighter than the traditional bean-laden rendition, but just as infused with flavor.

Serves 4–6

3 tablespoons canola oil

2 large onions, finely diced

6 garlic cloves, minced

1 red bell pepper, finely diced

1 green bell pepper, finely diced

1 ½ tablespoons chili powder

1 ½ teaspoons ground cumin

1 teaspoon dried oregano

5 cups water

1 (28-ounce) can imported plum tomatoes, finely chopped with their juice

¼ cup tomato paste, thinned with ¼ cup water

2 medium-large sweet potatoes (preferably yams), peeled and cut into ½-inch dice

2 (15-ounce) cans black beans, rinsed and well drained in a strainer

¾ teaspoon salt

Chopped cilantro or Sofrito (page 152) to taste for garnish (optional)

1. Heat the oil in a large stockpot over medium heat. Add the onions and garlic and sauté, stirring frequently, until the onions begin to brown, at least 10 minutes. Stir in the 2 bell peppers and cook 10 minutes, stirring often.

2. Sprinkle on the chili powder and cumin and cook the spices 2 minutes, stirring continuously. Stir in all the remaining ingredients—except the cilantro or Sofrito—and bring the mixture to a boil. Cook 15 minutes or so, or just until the sweet potatoes are tender. Stir the soup occasionally and be certain to scrape the bottom of the pot to dislodge any flavorful food bits that might be stuck there. Serve with some cilantro or Sofrito sprinkled on top, if desired.

Pizzas, Burgers, Sandwiches, Quesadillas, Etc.

Here is a hodgepodge of collations that can be just the right solution to those times when a full dinner seems too heavy and a salad is not quite enough. These are casual, fun foods that are eaten handheld. They can be extended with a salad or followed by a special dessert if you have the time and desire to make them, but could also suffice on their own. If you are having a friend over for lunch, choose something from this chapter to make it simple but special. What these meals lack in formality they make up in flavor.

See also: Mock Chicken Salad (page 212)
Curried Tofu "Eggless" Salad (page 213)
Barbecued Tempeh Spread (page 220)
Hummus (page 64)

Thin Crisp Tortilla Pizzas with Tomatoes and Goat Cheese

Using a flour tortilla as a base for pizza gives you an ultra-thin crust.

Serves 2–4

4 (8-inch) flour (wheat) tortillas
1¹/₂ tablespoons olive oil

The Topping
2¹/₂ cups grated part-skim mozzarella cheese
4 plum tomatoes, sliced
2 garlic cloves, minced
2 tablespoons olive oil
¹/₂ teaspoon dried basil
¹/₂ cup crumbled soft mild goat cheese

1. Preheat the oven to 375 degrees. Using 2 baking sheets, place 2 tortillas side by side on each sheet. With a pastry brush, lightly brush each tortilla with some of the olive oil. Flip the tortillas over and brush again. Bake 8–10 minutes, flipping over the tortillas and alternating the placement of the baking sheets halfway through the cooking time. Also, during the first few minutes, use a knife point to pop any air bubbles that might develop. The tortillas should be golden and crisp when done. (The tortillas may be prepared to this point up to 3 days in advance. Cool completely. Seal in a plastic bag and refrigerate until ready to use.)

2. Sprinkle the mozzarella evenly over the 4 tortillas. Place the tomatoes over the cheese.

3. Combine the garlic, olive oil, and basil and drizzle the mixture over the tomatoes.

4. Bake about 12 minutes, or until the cheese is bubbly. Alternate the placement of the baking sheets halfway during the cooking time. Remove the pizzas from the oven, then sprinkle bits of goat cheese all over their tops. Cut and serve immediately.

Tortilla Pizzas with Jalapeño Cheese and Roasted Peppers

The double impact of jalapeño peppers and blazing roasted red peppers electrifies these pizzas. A glass of cold beer alongside them would be welcome.

Serves 2–4

4 (8-inch) flour (wheat) tortillas
1 ½ tablespoons olive oil

The Topping
3 cups grated Monterey Jack cheese with jalapeño peppers
20 black olives (your favorite kind), pitted and halved (see page 95)
½ cup diced roasted red peppers, store-bought or freshly roasted (page 19)

1. Preheat the oven to 375 degrees. Prepare and precook the tortillas as for Thin Crisp Tortilla Pizzas with Tomatoes and Goat Cheese (step 1, opposite page).
2. Sprinkle the cheese on the tortillas. Top with the olives and peppers. Bake about 12 minutes, or until the cheese is bubbly. Alternate the placement of the baking sheets halfway during the cooking time. Cut and serve immediately.

Tortilla Pizzas with Feta Cheese, Zucchini, and Tomatoes

This could become a United Nations favorite—a Greek-style pizza on a tortilla! Three cultures represented in harmony.

Serves 2–4

4 (8-inch) flour (wheat) tortillas
1 ½ tablespoons olive oil

The Topping
4 plum tomatoes, thinly sliced
2 small zucchini, very thinly sliced
6 ounces (about 1 ⅓ cups) finely crumbled feta cheese
2 teaspoons dried oregano
3 tablespoons olive oil
Generous seasoning freshly ground black pepper

1. Preheat the oven to 375 degrees. Prepare and precook the tortillas as for Thin Crisp Tortilla Pizzas with Tomatoes and Goat Cheese (step 1, page 134).

2. Lay the tomato slices in one layer all over each tortilla. Spread the zucchini slices in one layer over the tomatoes (you might have some leftover zucchini slices).

3. In a medium-size bowl combine the feta cheese, oregano, olive oil, and pepper. Toss gently. With your fingers sprinkle the mixture evenly over the zucchini and tomato slices.

4. Bake about 12 minutes, or until the feta is sizzling and the zucchini is softened. Alternate the placement of the baking sheets halfway during the cooking time. Cut and serve immediately.

Beer Pizza

This pizza crust is a riot! My friend Geri Rybacki told me about this crust and I'm always amazed that it works so well. The beer lends the dough a yeasty flavor and contributes to its lightness. Just be certain to roll or pat it very thinly and cook it until golden brown.

Makes 2 (11–12-inch) pizzas

3 cups unbleached flour, plus extra for dusting
1 tablespoon baking powder
½ teaspoon salt
1 (12-ounce) bottle or can light or dark beer
Olive oil for greasing
3 cups grated part-skim mozzarella cheese
Toppings of your choice: diced tomatoes, garlic, sliced olives, mushrooms, peppers, etc.

1. Preheat the oven to 450 degrees. Combine the flour, baking powder, and salt in a large bowl and mix thoroughly. Pour in the beer and mix well. The dough will be sticky.
2. Spread a handful of flour on your work surface and dump the dough onto it. Toss the dough around to coat with the flour and prevent it from sticking. Knead it 2 or 3 times to make it pliable. Shape the dough into a ball, then divide it to make 2.
3. Lightly grease 2 baking sheets. Use a rolling pin to roll each ball into an 11- or 12-inch circle, or place the balls on the baking sheets and use your hands to flatten them into 11- or 12-inch circles. (If you are not ready to cook the pizza now, you can place the pans directly in the freezer to stop any rising action in the dough. Remove from the freezer about 30 minutes before cooking.)
4. I like to cook 1 pizza at a time, but you can cook the pizzas on 2 different oven racks and alternate them halfway through the cooking. Sprinkle 1½ cups of cheese on each crust. Top with the toppings of your choice. (Alternatively, you can make a traditional version with pizza sauce underneath the cheese—just be certain to spread a *thin* layer.)
5. Bake 12–15 minutes, or until golden brown on top and underneath.

Mixed Pepper Calzones

Calzones are essentially stuffed pizza turnovers. Frozen pizza dough works very well as a wrapping because it has a chance to get brown and chewy and so its texture is enhanced. If you can't get your hands on goat cheese, ricotta cheese is also delicious in these piquant calzones.

Makes 4 calzones

1 tablespoon olive oil, plus extra for brushing
1/8 teaspoon crushed red pepper flakes
1 green bell pepper, cut into thin 2-inch strips
1 red bell pepper, cut into thin 2-inch strips
1 medium onion, halved vertically and very thinly sliced
1/4 teaspoon dried thyme
Salt
Freshly ground black pepper to taste
1 cup (4 ounces) finely cubed part-skim mozzarella cheese
5 ounces soft mild goat cheese, crumbled
1 pound frozen bread (pizza) dough, thawed
Flour for dusting

1. Heat the tablespoon of oil in a large skillet over medium heat. Add the pepper flakes and cook 30 seconds. Mix in the 2 peppers, onion, thyme, salt, and pepper. Sauté the mixture, tossing often, until the vegetables are soft and brown, about 15 minutes. Scrape into a medium-size bowl and let cool completely. You can put it in the refrigerator or freezer to hasten the cooling, but keep an eye on it if you put it in the freezer so that it doesn't freeze.

2. When the mixture is cooled stir in the 2 cheeses. Preheat the oven to 375 degrees. Lightly grease a baking sheet.

3. Divide the pizza dough in four and roll each portion into a ball. Place a small bowl of

water in front of you. Dust your work surface with a little flour. With a rolling pin roll a ball of dough into a 7-inch circle, dusting the dough with flour as necessary. Dip your finger in the water and moisten the outer edge of the dough circle. Place one quarter of the pepper-cheese mixture on half of the dough, then fold the remaining dough over to make a turnover. Carefully pinch together and fold over the edges of the dough to make a tight seal. Repeat with the remaining 3 portions.

4. Place the calzones on the baking sheet. With your fingers lightly coat the top of each calzone with a little oil. Bake 25 minutes, or until golden brown. Let sit at least 10 minutes before serving, for they will be too hot to eat before then.

Spicy Garlic and Potato Calzones

Potatoes and garlic are a match made in heaven. The potatoes soak up this garlicky sauté and come to life, making a delectable filling. Calzones reheat extremely well, so if you have any left over, you can look forward to them for another lunch or dinner.

Makes 4

2 ¼ cups diced (¼ inch) peeled boiling potatoes (about 2 medium-large)

2 tablespoons olive oil, plus extra for brushing

4 fat garlic cloves, minced

¼ teaspoon crushed red pepper flakes

1 tomato, cored, seeded, and finely cubed

Generous seasoning salt

1 cup (4 ounces) finely cubed part-skim mozzarella cheese

Flour for dusting

1 pound frozen bread (pizza) dough, thawed

1. Place the potatoes in a large skillet with about 2 inches of water. Cover the pan and bring to a boil. Reduce to a simmer and cook until the potatoes are tender, about 10 minutes. Drain the potatoes in a colander.

2. Wipe the skillet clean, then pour in the 2 tablespoons olive oil. Place over medium heat. Add the garlic and crushed red pepper flakes and cook 30 seconds. Mix in the tomato and cook, tossing often, until the tomato is soft, about 2 minutes. Stir in the potatoes, season generously with salt, and cook another 2 minutes, or until the mixture is hot and sizzling. Remove from the heat and cool completely. (This mixture can be prepared up to 8 hours in advance.)

3. When the mixture is cool stir in the mozzarella cheese. Preheat the oven to 375 degrees. Lightly grease a baking sheet.

4. Lightly flour your work surface. Place a small bowl of water in front of you. Divide the pizza dough into 4 and roll each portion into a ball. With a rolling pin roll a ball of dough

into a 7-inch circle, lightly dusting the dough with some flour as necessary to prevent sticking. Dip your finger in the water and moisten the edge of the circle. Place one quarter of the potato mixture on half the circle, then fold the remaining dough over the mixture to make a turnover. Carefully pinch and fold over the edges of the dough to make a tight seal. Repeat with the remaining 3 portions.

5. Place the calzones on the baking sheet. With your fingers lightly coat the top of each calzone with a little oil. Bake 30 minutes, or until deep golden brown. Let sit at least 10 minutes before biting into one because otherwise it will release a blast of hot steam and scald you.

Black Bean and Red Onion Burgers

Salsa mayonnaise is the perfect topping for these delicious burgers, but if you want to go the whole hog, add sliced red onion and lettuce for an extra kick.

Makes 3 burgers

2 cups freshly cooked or canned black beans, rinsed and well drained if canned

1 egg, beaten

⅓ cup minced red onion

1 teaspoon chili powder

⅓ cup dry bread crumbs

⅓ cup mayonnaise

⅓ cup salsa (mild, medium, or hot)

Oil for frying

3 burger rolls

1. Place the beans in a medium-size bowl and mash about two thirds of them with a fork. Stir in the egg, onion, chili powder, and bread crumbs. Cover and chill for 30 minutes, or up to 24 hours.

2. Meanwhile place the mayonnaise in a small cup and stir until smooth. (This advance stirring prevents lumps from forming when the salsa is stirred in.) Stir in the salsa. Chill 30 minutes.

3. Form the burger mixture into 3 patties. Cook in a lightly oiled frying pan until golden brown on each side and piping hot throughout, at least 10 minutes total.

4. Serve the burgers on rolls with some salsa mayonnaise spread on each half.

Herbed Bean Burgers

Poultry seasoning lends these burgers a flavor reminiscent of traditional stuffing. They pair well with Russian dressing (mayonnaise with a little ketchup and relish) as a topping; however, mayonnaise alone is also a good match. And for the crowning touch? Lettuce and tomato, of course, to make an impressive, towering burger.

Makes 3 burgers

2 cups freshly cooked or canned white beans (such as navy, Great Northern, or cannellini), rinsed and well drained if canned

$\frac{1}{4}$ cup minced celery

$\frac{1}{4}$ cup minced red onion

1 garlic clove, put through a press or minced

$\frac{1}{2}$ cup dry bread crumbs

$\frac{1}{2}$ teaspoon poultry seasoning

1 teaspoon red wine vinegar

1 teaspoon tamari soy sauce

Salt

Generous seasoning freshly ground black pepper

Oil for frying or grilling

3 burger rolls

1. Place the beans in a medium-size bowl and mash half of them with a fork. Stir in all the remaining ingredients, except the oil and burger rolls, then use your hands to knead it all together into a ball.

2. Form the mixture into 3 burgers. If you are not going to cook them right away, you can wrap them individually in plastic wrap and refrigerate up to 4 days. Grill or fry them on a lightly oiled grill or skillet over medium heat until golden on both sides and hot throughout. Serve them on round rolls with Russian dressing, lettuce, and sliced tomato.

Shiitake Mushroom, Roasted Red Pepper, and Arugula Sandwiches

I had a sandwich with this combination at The Union Bar and Grill in Great Barrington, Massachusetts, and I knew I had to re-create it at home. The wedding of these ingredients is a triumph of flavor, texture, and color, but you must use high-quality, homemade-type bread to successfully hold it all together. I "roast" the shiitakes and onion in a hot oven; however, if you have a grill, by all means cook them on that.

Makes 2 sandwiches

2 tablespoons olive oil

1 teaspoon tamari soy sauce

1 medium red onion, sliced into $\frac{1}{2}$-inch-thick slices and separated into rings

8 medium shiitake mushrooms, stems discarded and caps wiped clean

Salt

Freshly ground black pepper

4 slices homemade-type bread, such as sourdough, Tuscan, or semolina bread

1 roasted red pepper, cut in half, either freshly roasted (page 19) or store-bought

8 large arugula leaves (approximately)

1. Preheat the oven to 450 degrees. In a medium-size bowl combine the oil and tamari. Add the onion rings, shiitakes, salt, and pepper and toss to coat. Lay the vegetables on a roasting pan or baking sheet in one layer. Roast until brown and juicy, about 10–15 minutes. Flip the mushrooms over halfway during the cooking time.

2. Top 2 of the bread slices with the mushroom-onion mixture. Lay a red pepper half and some of the arugula on each sandwich. Top with the remaining bread, then slice each sandwich in half.

Portobello Mushroom, Smothered Onion, and Feta Cheese Sandwiches

The onions and mushrooms in this sandwich are natural mates. Choose a good-quality baguette to make this a sensational sandwich.

Serves 2

½ tablespoon unsalted butter

2 large portobello mushrooms, stems discarded and caps wiped clean

2 (¼-inch-thick) red onion slices

2 tablespoons olive oil

1 teaspoon red wine vinegar

Salt

Generous seasoning freshly ground black pepper

2 pieces French bread, each approximately 5 inches long

3 tablespoons crumbled feta cheese

1. Melt the butter in a large skillet over medium heat. Add the mushroom caps and cook 10 minutes or so, or until they begin to get juicy.

2. Separate the onion slices into rings and add to the mushrooms. Cover the pan, then cook until the onions are very soft and the mushrooms are juicy throughout, about 10 minutes. Occasionally remove the cover and toss the ingredients so they cook evenly. Remove from the heat.

3. In a small bowl mix together the olive oil, vinegar, salt, and pepper.

4. Slice the French bread horizontally. Spoon the olive oil mixture on both sides of each pair. Sprinkle the feta cheese on the bottom halves. Top with the mushrooms and onions, then the remaining bread.

Fried Green Tomato, Basil, and Smoked Cheese Sandwiches

Cornmeal-encrusted fried-tomato slices have a semblance of meatiness that reminds me of eggplant. Paired with basil and smoked cheese you have the workings of a vegetarian BLT—albeit, totally transformed!

Makes 2 sandwiches

2 tablespoons cornmeal

Salt

Freshly ground black pepper

1 medium green tomato, cut into ¼-inch-thick slices

Oil for frying

Mayonnaise

4 slices crusty white bread (preferably Tuscan-style or sourdough)

2 thin slices (about 1 ounce) smoked cheese (such as mozzarella or Gouda)

8 basil leaves

1. Combine the cornmeal, salt, and pepper on a small plate. Dip the green tomato slices in the mixture and thoroughly coat both sides of each slice.

2. Heat just enough oil over moderate heat in a medium-size skillet to coat the bottom of the pan. Fry the tomato slices until they are golden brown on each side and tender, about 10 minutes. Let cool to warm.

3. Spread a thin layer of mayonnaise on each bread slice and top two of the slices with some cheese, basil leaves, and the fried tomatoes. Form into 2 sandwiches and slice each in half.

Broccoli and
Jalapeño Cheese Quesadillas

You'll love these scrumptious quesadillas and the fact that they are assembled with so few ingredients. They can be easily doubled, tripled, etc., so don't hesitate to serve them to a crowd.

Serves 2

2 stalks broccoli (to yield 3½ cups chopped broccoli)
4 (8-inch) flour (wheat) tortillas
1½ cups grated Monterey Jack cheese with jalapeño peppers

1. Peel the stalks of the broccoli, then finely chop the stalks and florets.

2. Steam the broccoli until tender—neither crunchy nor mushy. Drain well and let cool.

3. To assemble, place 2 tortillas on a counter. Sprinkle one quarter of the cheese on each tortilla, leaving empty a 1-inch border around the tortilla. Spread *half* the broccoli on each tortilla. Sprinkle the remaining cheese on the broccoli, then place the remaining tortillas on top to create a sandwich. Press down with your hands to help the quesadillas stick together.

4. You can either cook the quesadillas on the stove top or in the oven. To cook them on the stove top, place 1 quesadilla on a large, ungreased skillet (if your tortillas are fresh and moist) or on a lightly buttered skillet (if the tortillas are on the dry side) and cook, over medium heat, for about 10 minutes, flipping with a spatula after the first 5 minutes. If you prefer to bake your quesadillas, place them on an ungreased baking sheet (or a lightly buttered one if your tortillas are somewhat dry), and bake in a preheated 375-degree oven for about 10 minutes, flipping the quesadillas over after 5 minutes. Whether cooked in a skillet or oven, the quesadillas are done when they begin to get brown flecks on them and the cheese is melted. Place the quesadillas on a cutting board and cut into 4 wedges. Let them rest a little before serving because they will be piping hot.

Corn, Black Bean, and Red Onion Quesadillas

I always have these ingredients on hand, and so these quesadillas are often what come to mind when I'm searching for a quick lunch or dinner. Kidney beans work just as well as black beans so don't hesitate to make that substitution if it suits you.

Serves 2

4 (8-inch) flour (wheat) tortillas

½ cup frozen corn, thawed

½ cup freshly cooked or canned black beans, rinsed and well drained if canned

⅓ cup paper-thin slivers of red onion

1 cup grated Monterey Jack cheese

½ teaspoon chili powder

1. Place 2 tortillas in front of you on a work surface. Sprinkle *half* the corn, beans, onion, cheese, and chili powder evenly on *each* tortilla, leaving a 1-inch border around the tortilla. Top with the remaining tortillas to create "sandwiches," and press down on the quesadillas to help them stick together.

2. You can either cook the quesadillas on the stove top or in the oven. To cook them on the stove top, place 1 quesadilla on a large, ungreased skillet (if your tortillas are fresh and moist) or on a lightly buttered skillet (if the tortillas are on the dry side) and cook, over medium heat, for about 10 minutes, flipping with a spatula after the first 5 minutes. If you prefer to bake your quesadillas, place them on an ungreased baking sheet (or a lightly buttered one if your tortillas are somewhat dry), and bake in a preheated 375-degree oven for about 10 minutes, flipping the quesadillas over after 5 minutes. Whether cooked in a skillet or oven, the quesadillas are done when they begin to get brown flecks on them and the cheese is melted. Place the quesadillas on a cutting board and cut into 4 wedges. Let them rest a little before serving because they will be piping hot.

Zucchini, Tomato, and Mozzarella Quesadillas

I choose a plum tomato for this filling because it is less juicy and more meaty than a round tomato. If your tomato is too ripe and juicy (a problem that is conceivable only in August or September), it could make these quesadillas a tad messy to eat. However, I'm sure you'll love them nonetheless.

Serves 2

4 (8-inch) flour (wheat) tortillas
1 ¼ cups grated part-skim mozzarella cheese
1 small zucchini, very thinly sliced
1 plum tomato, very thinly sliced
2 tablespoons shredded basil, or ½ teaspoon dried

1. Place two tortillas side by side on a countertop. Sprinkle one quarter of the cheese on each tortilla. Layer *half* the zucchini slices, tomato slices, and basil onto each tortilla, then sprinkle on the remaining cheese. Top with the remaining tortillas to make a "sandwich."

2. You can either cook the quesadillas on the stove top or in the oven. To cook them on the stove top, place 1 quesadilla on a large, ungreased skillet (if your tortillas are fresh and moist) or on a lightly buttered skillet (if the tortillas are on the dry side) and cook, over medium heat, for about 10 minutes, flipping with a spatula after the first 5 minutes. If you prefer to bake your quesadillas, place them on an ungreased baking sheet (or a lightly buttered one if your tortillas are somewhat dry), and bake in a preheated 375-degree oven for about 10 minutes, flipping the quesadillas over after 5 minutes. Whether cooked in a skillet or oven, the quesadillas are done when they begin to get brown flecks on them and the cheese is melted. Place the quesadillas on a cutting board and cut into 4 wedges. Let them rest a little before serving because they will be piping hot.

Portobello Mushroom Quesadillas

The pure experience of chewy, meaty portobellos comes through in these simple yet distinguished quesadillas. Think of these the next time you want an easy finger food for an appetizer. For such an occasion, just cut them into 8 instead of 4 portions.

Serves 2

1 tablespoon unsalted butter

3 medium-large (1 pound weight with stems) portobello mushrooms, stems discarded and caps thinly sliced

2 scallions, very thinly sliced

Salt

Freshly ground black pepper

4 (8-inch) flour (wheat) tortillas

1¼ cups grated Muenster cheese

1. Melt the butter in a large skillet over medium heat. Add the mushrooms and sauté them, tossing often, until they are brown and juicy and their juices begin to evaporate, at least 10 minutes. Make certain they are cooked throughout. Remove the pan from the heat, mix in the scallions, salt, and pepper. Let the mixture cool to room temperature.

2. To assemble the quesadillas, place 2 tortillas on a counter. Sprinkle one quarter of the cheese on *each* tortilla, leaving an empty 1-inch border around the edges. Spread *half* the mushroom filling on each tortilla, then top with the remaining cheese. Place the remaining tortillas on top to create "sandwiches." Press down with your hands to help the quesadillas stick together.

3. You can either cook the quesadillas on the stove top or in the oven. To cook them on the stove top, place 1 quesadilla on a large, ungreased skillet (if your tortillas are fresh and moist) or on a lightly buttered skillet (if the tortillas are on the dry side) and cook, over medium heat, for about 10 minutes, flipping with a spatula after the first 5 minutes. If you prefer to bake your quesadillas, place them on an ungreased baking sheet (or a

lightly buttered one if your tortillas are somewhat dry), and bake in a preheated 375-degree oven for about 10 minutes, flipping the quesadillas over after 5 minutes. Whether cooked in a skillet or oven, the quesadillas are done when they begin to get brown flecks on them and the cheese is melted. Place the quesadillas on a cutting board and cut into 4 wedges. Let them rest a little before serving because they will be piping hot.

Quesadillas

Quesadillas are best described as Mexican grilled cheese sandwiches made with 2 flour tortillas or 1 tortilla folded in half. They are usually fried in oil, butter, or lard, but I find them much more delicious and less greasy if cooked on a dry pan. (If you are not able to find flaky, supple tortillas, however, you will probably need to put a little butter in the skillet or on your baking pan when cooking your quesadilla to help soften the tortillas.)

Quesadillas can be the ideal vehicle for a quick supper or lunch because you can improvise with different cheeses and vegetables and come up with delectable fillings. There is one caveat, however, and that is you *must* use high-quality tortillas if you want good results. All flour tortillas are *not* alike; in fact, some are more like cardboard than bread. I have found a brand, called Maria and Ricardo's (from Jamaica Plain, Massachusetts), that is fantastic. Their tortillas are chewy and flaky, and delicious just heated and eaten with a little butter. So do experiment with different brands until you find a good one, then always keep a few packages in your freezer for convenience.

The next time you have an informal party or large get-together consider making a few different fillings and serving quesadillas at the gathering. Use 2 baking sheets at once and reverse their positions in the oven midway through the cooking time. Serve with a tossed salad and you have a delicious meal for a crowd.

Bean Tostadas with Sofrito

I have always been lukewarm toward cilantro; I could take it or leave it. Then a friend of mine, Geri Rybacki, dropped off a container of what she called "Puerto Rican sofrito," and my taste buds have never been the same. Geri pureed her sofrito to the point where it resembled a pesto, and we liked it so much in its raw state that we never got to use it in the traditional manner.

The point of departure from more familiar pestos is the addition of vinegar. This makes all the flavors come alive and lends a special "pickled" nuance to the sauce.

Serves 3

Sofrito

3–4 cups lightly packed cilantro, stems included, washed and spun dry

1 small jalapeño pepper, seeded and chopped (wear rubber gloves)

1 small green bell pepper, cored and chopped

2 garlic cloves, minced

1 small onion, chopped

$\frac{1}{3}$ cup olive oil

$\frac{1}{4}$ cup cider vinegar

$\frac{1}{2}$ teaspoon salt

The Beans

1 (16-ounce) can pinto or kidney beans, rinsed well and drained

1 teaspoon chili powder

$\frac{1}{4}$ cup water

$\frac{1}{4}$ teaspoon salt

The Tortillas

6 small (6-inch) soft corn tortillas

2–3 tablespoons canola oil

$\frac{2}{3}$ cup grated Monterey Jack cheese

1. To make the sofrito, combine all of the sofrito ingredients in a food processor or blender and puree until smooth. Pour into a container with a cover and set aside.

2. To prepare the beans, combine them with the chili powder, water, and salt in the container of a food processor and puree. Scrape into a bowl.

3. Preheat the broiler. Brush both sides of each tortilla with some of the oil, and place the tortillas on a baking sheet. (You'll probably have to do this in batches.) Broil on both sides until golden and crisp. (The tortillas may be prepared to this point up to 24 hours in advance.)

4. Divide the bean mixture and spread some on each tortilla. Top each with some of the grated cheese. Broil the tostadas until the cheese has melted and they are hot throughout. Serve with little spoonfuls of sofrito dotted on the top of each tostada.

Note: This recipe makes an ample amount of sofrito. Use the leftover sauce on rice dishes, in soups and chilis, and on other Mexican-style bean creations.

Side Dishes

There are occasions when a special side dish would nicely round out the meal, such as alongside savory tarts, egg dishes, or as part of a large holiday spread. But why wait for the need to arise to serve a sumptuous potato dish such as Garlic Mashed Potatoes (page 156) or Scalloped Potatoes and Onions (page 158)? You can always accompany it with some Roasted Vegetables (page 163), for example, and fashion a meal out of two smashing side dishes, with perhaps a salad and some bread to precede them.

So whether you are looking for that "extra something" to balance a menu, or want to bring together favorite side dishes to create an entree, these memorable accompaniments will help you with your meal planning.

Garlic Mashed Potatoes

Some people prefer "baking" potatoes for mashed potato dishes because they are light in texture; however, I like the creaminess that results from using starchy, boiling potatoes. Also, I like to whip my potatoes using an electric hand mixer, although some have claimed this makes them gummy. I have never found this to be true. *Chacun à son goût.* This version of garlic mashed potatoes calls for simmering the garlic in the milk that is added when whipping the potatoes. It mellows the garlic while still imparting its unmistakable flavor. You won't have any leftovers with these luscious potatoes.

Serves 4 very generously (as they should be served)

1¼ cups milk, plus more if necessary
6 large garlic cloves, peeled and coarsely chopped
5 large (3 pounds) boiling (waxy) potatoes, peeled and quartered
2 tablespoons unsalted butter
½ teaspoon salt
Freshly ground black pepper

1. Combine the milk and garlic in a medium-size, heavy-bottomed saucepan and bring it to a simmer. Simmer about 20 minutes, or until the garlic is very soft. Keep an eye on the pot to prevent the milk from swelling and boiling over; it should cook at just a simmer.

2. Meanwhile boil the potatoes in a large pot of water until they are tender when pierced with a knife.

3. While the potatoes are cooking puree the garlic and milk in a blender just until smooth. Return the garlic cream to the pot. (You can do this step up to a few hours before cooking the potatoes.)

4. Drain the potatoes in a colander, then return them to the pot over low heat. Add the garlic cream, butter, salt, and pepper. With an electric mixer whip the potatoes until creamy. Serve immediately or cover and keep warm over low heat.

Baked Chive and
Mashed Potato Casserole

So many mashed potato dishes need to be served immediately because they suffer from reheating. This version is ideal for entertaining because not only is it exceptionally light and savory but it can be made up to 8 hours in advance of baking it.

Serves 8

3 pounds (5 large) boiling (waxy) potatoes, peeled and quartered

2 tablespoons unsalted butter cut into bits, plus extra for greasing

6 ounces whipped cream cheese with chives

2 eggs

½ teaspoon salt

Freshly ground black pepper

2 tablespoons grated Parmesan cheese

1. Boil the potatoes in a large stockpot until they are tender when pierced with a knife. Drain thoroughly and return them to the pot.

2. Add the butter and stir to melt. Drop in the cream cheese, eggs, salt, and pepper. With an electric mixer whip the potatoes until fluffy.

3. Lightly butter a 2-quart shallow casserole. Spoon the potato mixture into it and smooth over the top. Sprinkle with the Parmesan cheese. (The casserole may be prepared to this point up to 8 hours in advance. If made more than 2 hours in advance, cover with foil and refrigerate it. Bring to room temperature before baking.)

4. Preheat the oven to 400 degrees. Bake the casserole, uncovered, for 40 minutes, or until golden on top and sizzling.

Scalloped Potatoes and Onions

Here's a light version of scalloped potatoes that's just as delicious as the traditional dish. Serve it as a side dish or as a hearty, main-course casserole, accompanied by a salad to round out the meal. The onions will be brown and caramelized, the top of the dish golden and crusty—just as you would expect of that classic potato gratin.

Serves 6

3 tablespoons unsalted butter, plus extra for greasing
2 large onions, halved vertically and thinly sliced
1½ cups vegetable stock, store-bought or homemade (page 13)
5 large (3 pounds) boiling potatoes
1½ cups grated cheese, preferably Swiss or Cheddar
Salt and freshly ground pepper to taste

1. Melt 1 tablespoon butter in a large skillet over medium heat. Add the onions and sauté, stirring often, until they begin to get brown, about 10 minutes. Set aside.

2. Lightly butter a shallow 2½-quart ovenproof casserole or oval gratin dish. Set it aside. Place the vegetable stock in a large bowl. Peel, then rinse, the potatoes. Slice each potato in half vertically, then very thinly into half moons. Drop them into the vegetable stock as you slice them. This prevents them from turning brown and allows you to postpone cooking the casserole. You can keep them in the stock, stirring occasionally, for up to 4 hours.

3. Preheat the oven to 425 degrees. Spoon half the potatoes into the prepared casserole in an even layer. Spread the onions on top. Cut 1 tablespoon of the butter into bits and layer on top of the onion. Sprinkle on *half* of the grated cheese. Add salt and pepper.

4. Spoon on the remaining potatoes, then pour all the stock over everything. Top with the remaining tablespoon of butter cut into bits, then season again with salt and pepper.

5. Bake 30 minutes. Remove the casserole from the oven and flatten the top with the back of a spatula. Sprinkle on the remaining cheese. Bake 30 more minutes, or until the potatoes are tender, and the top is brown and crusty. Let sit 10 minutes before serving.

Roasted Home Fries

These little roasted potato disks are so quick and easy to prepare, they're bound to become your favorite method of making home fries. I have had great results baking these potatoes at different temperatures, depending on whether or not the oven needed to be set at a specific temperature for another dish. Just don't go lower than 350 degrees because you need that much heat to brown them. If you have another dish baking at the time you want to cook these, bake these home fries on the lower rack.

Serves 4–6

6 medium-large red-skinned potatoes
2 tablespoons olive oil
Salt

1. Preheat the oven to 425 degrees. Peel the potatoes, then slice them ¼ inch thick. Cut the slices in half so that each piece is about the size of a half dollar. Place the potatoes on a large baking sheet. Drizzle the oil all over them, then with your hands, toss to coat them thoroughly with the oil.

2. Bake about 25 minutes (or longer if the oven is at a lower setting), tossing them once after the first 15 minutes. When done, they will be tender and golden all over. Season with salt before serving.

Sweet Potato and
Red Pepper Home Fries

Roasting these "home fries" causes their sugars to caramelize and make them brown and crispy on the edges. The vibrant splash of color this combination provides looks terrific next to a slice of frittata or simple scrambled eggs.

Although I usually cook these vegetables at a high oven setting, they are successful in an oven as low as 350 degrees; you'll just have to cook them about 10 minutes longer. This sometimes is necessary if you are baking something simultaneously that requires the lower oven setting.

Serves 4–6

3 medium sweet potatoes or yams, peeled, quartered, and sliced $\frac{1}{4}$ inch thick

1 medium red bell pepper, cut into pieces $2 \times \frac{1}{2}$ inch

1 large onion, halved vertically and sliced $\frac{1}{4}$ inch thick

2 tablespoons olive oil

1 tablespoon tamari soy sauce

Freshly ground black pepper

1. Preheat the oven to 425 degrees. Combine all the ingredients in a large bowl and toss well to evenly coat with the oil and soy sauce.

2. Spread the vegetables on a large baking sheet or roasting pan so that they rest in one layer. When the oven is thoroughly preheated, bake the vegetables for 30 minutes, removing the pan from the oven and tossing them once at the halfway point. When done, the vegetables should be tender and brown.

Whipped Sweet Potatoes

A satin-like consistency and spicy flavor make these sweet potatoes an outstanding side dish. Remember them for your next Thanksgiving feast.

Serves 4 generously

4 medium-large (2 pounds) yams or sweet potatoes
3 tablespoons unsalted butter
¼ cup pure maple syrup
¼ cup heavy cream
¼ teaspoon ground cinnamon
⅛ teaspoon ground allspice
Salt
Freshly ground black pepper

1. Peel the yams or sweet potatoes and cut them into 1-inch dice. Place them in a 3-quart saucepan and fill with water to cover. Partly cover the pan and bring to a boil. Cook until the sweet potatoes are very tender, about 15 minutes. Drain in a colander.

2. While the potatoes are draining, quickly heat the remaining ingredients in the same saucepan until the mixture is hot and the ingredients are combined. Remove the pan from the heat and stir in the sweet potatoes.

3. With a handheld electric mixer whip the sweet potatoes until smooth. (You could, alternatively, do this step in a food processor and then reheat the potatoes until hot.)

4. Serve immediately, or keep covered over low heat until serving time.

Roasted Vegetables

This side dish of roasted vegetables is quite versatile. It can be made in advance and reheated; used as a sandwich filling on French bread; incorporated into a frittata or omelet; or just served alongside Garlic Mashed Potatoes (page 156) for a dynamic combination.

Serves 4 generously

1 green or red bell pepper, cored and cut into ½-inch dice

2 small–medium zucchini, quartered lengthwise and cut into ½-inch dice

1 small (1 pound) eggplant, sliced lengthwise and cut into ½-inch dice

1 large onion, cut into ½-inch dice

2 plum tomatoes, cored, seeded, and cut into 1-inch dice

3 garlic cloves, minced

¼ teaspoon dried rosemary, finely crumbled

2 tablespoons olive oil

1 teaspoon tamari soy sauce

Generous seasoning freshly ground black pepper

Salt

1. Preheat the oven to 425 degrees. Combine all the vegetables plus the garlic and rosemary in a large bowl. Mix together the olive oil and tamari and pour over the vegetables. Toss well.

2. Spread the vegetables on a large baking sheet in one layer. Season generously with pepper. Bake 30 minutes, tossing once after 15 minutes. The vegetables will be very tender when done, not crunchy. Season with salt just before serving.

Roasted Asparagus

I thought I had tried every conceivable way to cook asparagus until my friend Jane Walsh told me how fabulous they are when roasted. If you want a side dish of plain asparagus that is highly flavorful without any doctoring, choose this method. Just be sure to remove the tough bottoms of the asparagus by cutting off the white part, then peeling the bottom 2 inches. This will produce perfectly tender, succulent asparagus.

Serves 4

1 pound asparagus

1 ½ tablespoons olive oil (approximately)

Salt (preferably coarse kosher salt)

1. Preheat the oven to 425 degrees. Cut off the white bottoms of the asparagus and discard them. With a sharp paring knife peel the bottom 2–3 inches of the asparagus to remove any tough skin.

2. Place the asparagus in a roasting pan or on a baking sheet and drizzle the olive oil all over them. With your hands roll the asparagus around so they are evenly coated with the oil. Sprinkle with salt to taste.

3. Bake about 10 minutes, or until tender when pierced with a knife.

Couscous Pilaf with Pistachio Nuts and Scallions

This light and flavorsome side dish of couscous goes well with assertive entrees, such as Baked Thai-Style Tofu (page 215). You can successfully make this pilaf in advance and reheat it in the oven in a foil-covered dish. Just sprinkle it with a few teaspoons of water to help create steam.

Serves 4

1 tablespoon unsalted butter
1 large scallion, thinly sliced
1 ½ cups vegetable stock, store-bought or homemade (page 13)
¼ teaspoon salt
1 cup couscous
⅓ cup shelled pistachio nuts

1. Melt the butter in a small- or medium-size saucepan over medium heat. Add the scallion and sauté 30 seconds. Pour in the vegetable stock and salt and bring to a boil.
2. Mix in the couscous and pistachio nuts and cover the pan. Remove it from the heat and let sit 5 minutes. Fluff with a fork, cover, and let sit 2–10 minutes more.

Coconut Lime Rice

I am quite fond of this aromatic pilaf and so sometimes make a simple meal by just serving it alongside a steamed vegetable, such as green beans.

Serves 4

2 tablespoons unsalted butter
1 onion, very finely diced
1 cup basmati rice or converted white rice
1 $^3/_4$ cups water
$^1/_2$ teaspoon salt
2 tablespoons sliced almonds
2 tablespoons desiccated unsweetened coconut (see Note)
$^1/_4$ teaspoon ground cardamom
Juice of $^1/_2$ lime

1. Melt 1 tablespoon of the butter in a medium-size saucepan over medium heat. Add the onion and sauté until tender, about 5 minutes.
2. Stir in the rice and cook 1 minute, stirring continuously, then add the water and salt. Raise the heat to high, cover the pan, and bring the contents to a boil. Reduce the heat to a simmer and cook until all the water is absorbed, about 18–20 minutes.
3. Meanwhile melt the remaining tablespoon of butter in a small skillet over medium heat. Stir in the almonds and sauté 2 minutes, or just until the almonds are faintly colored. Add the coconut and cardamom and cook until the coconut begins to get a light golden color, about 1 minute. Remove from the heat.
4. When the rice has absorbed all the water, very gently stir in the almond mixture and lime juice. Remove from the heat and let sit, covered, 5–10 minutes.

Note: Desiccated unsweetened coconut can be purchased at natural foods stores and some specialty markets.

Frittatas and Omelets

The debate continues on whether eggs are a perfect food, that is, a good source of protein, vitamins, and minerals, or whether they should be marked with a scarlet letter and shunned because of their high cholesterol content. Depending on when and where you read the latest research, you'll hear many conflicting perspectives. Several recent comprehensive scientific studies indicate that blood cholesterol is not elevated by dietary cholesterol, and therefore a moderate consumption of eggs poses no problem for generally healthy adults.

I suspect this is the most reasonable approach to take toward the much maligned egg, and so a couple of times a month I serve an omelet or frittata to my family for dinner and we enjoy it wholeheartedly. I do always purchase organic eggs, however, because I don't want the hormones and antibiotics that factory-farmed chickens ingest. Eggs are an inexpensive food to begin with, so I don't mind the extra cost of purchasing eggs that come from free-range chickens.

Making an omelet is one of the simplest and quickest of tasks to perform at the stove, yet it is also quite easy to make a mess of it. A non-stick skillet will help things considerably; however, a heavy-bottomed omelet pan will work well if enough oil or butter is used to prevent the omelet from sticking.

It's a good idea to make 1 omelet at a time because you'll have more control of the process. With 40 seconds the average time it takes to complete the task, individual omelet making will not delay your dinner.

The key to a tender, delicate omelet is to use high heat and a quick hand. When your pan is hot and the oil or butter starts to sizzle, it is ready for the eggs. Pour in the beaten eggs and watch them immediately begin to set at the edges. Use an inverted spatula to push in the edges and cause the uncooked eggs to spill over onto the pan. When very little uncooked egg remains visible, spoon on your *hot* filling, then fold over the omelet and slide it onto your plate. This should all take under 1 minute.

If the filling for your omelet is more than grated cheese, that is, a cooked vegetable concoction, make certain it is hot when you spoon it onto the omelet. You can keep it warm on the back burner while you cook your eggs.

A tiny bit of water is beaten into the eggs to lighten their texture and help steam them during cooking; however, you can also use club soda or white wine to do the trick.

Frittatas

The Italian version of an omelet, known as a frittata, combines the filling ingredients with the beaten eggs and cooks them together to form a firm, pie-shaped egg dish. In contrast to the French omelet, frittatas should be cooked slowly over low or medium-low heat.

A non-stick skillet is ideal because the frittata will be easy to remove from the pan. Heating a small amount of butter or oil in the pan before the egg mixture is poured in will add flavor and facilitate the removal of the frittata. I used to bemoan the fact that my skillet had a plastic handle and, therefore, was unsafe to put under the broiler. Now I know a handy trick that cleverly solves the problem: Just wrap a double layer of foil around the handle to protect it from the heating element and broil away!

Frittatas can also be successfully baked rather than cooked on the stove top. This method can be a lifesaver if you are preparing a brunch, for example, where a number of dishes will be cooked on the burners. To bake a frittata, butter a pie plate (such as a Pyrex 9-inch pie dish) and pour in the egg mixture. Bake it in a preheated 350-degree oven for 20–30 minutes, or until it is no longer runny on top. (The temperature of the added vegetable mixture affects the cooking time. If the vegetables are quite warm rather than at room temperature, the frittata won't take as long to cook.) Keep an eye on it to prevent overcooking. You don't need to broil the top of the frittata when you use the baking method.

Think of frittatas when you are planning a picnic, as the French and Italians do. They are delicious cold or at room temperature, and they travel well.

Leek, Fennel, and Goat Cheese Frittata

Here's a frittata that's fit for a special occasion. The creamy pockets of goat cheese along with this triumphant blending of flavors make this egg dish ideal for a no-fuss, yet memorable meal. It can be easily doubled, and in that case, you'd need a 10-inch skillet. Just be certain to cook the frittata on low heat as directed; this will produce very tender results.

Serves 2

1 tablespoon unsalted butter
1½ cups thinly sliced fennel (about ½ large bulb)
1 leek, halved lengthwise, washed thoroughly, and thinly sliced
1 plum tomato, diced
4 large eggs
¼ teaspoon salt
Generous seasoning freshly ground black pepper
2 ounces soft mild goat cheese, crumbled

1. Over medium heat melt the butter in an 8-inch non-stick skillet, and roll it around so the butter coats the sides. Add the fennel and sauté until tender, about 10 minutes.

2. Stir in the leek and tomato and cook, stirring often, until the leek is soft, about 10 minutes. At first the vegetables will crowd the pan, but they will shrink once cooked. You can prepare the vegetables in advance to this point, then reheat before beginning step 3.

3. Meanwhile beat the eggs thoroughly. Add the salt, pepper, and crumbled goat cheese and stir very gently to keep the goat cheese in separate pieces rather than completely blended into the egg mixture.

4. When the vegetables are cooked, reduce the heat to a low setting. Carefully pour in the egg mixture and stir gently to incorporate it. Cook slowly until the eggs are almost set, about 15 minutes. During this time use a rubber spatula to loosen the edges of the

frittata and let some of the liquid egg fall over the sides onto the pan. This will help it cook more evenly. Meanwhile turn on the broiler.

5. When the frittata is about 80 percent set and there is just a film of uncooked egg on top, broil it for 1 minute or so, or until set. Do not overcook it. (If your skillet doesn't have an ovenproof handle, wrap a double layer of foil around it before placing it under the broiler.) Cut the frittata in half and serve immediately.

Spinach, Potato, and Feta Cheese Frittata

The saltiness of the feta cheese becomes subdued in this frittata yet retains its tangy character to give this frittata some spunk. Serve hot pita bread alongside it for a good match.

Serves 2

½ pound fresh spinach in a bunch, or ½ (10-ounce) bag fresh spinach, stems removed and leaves torn (5 cups leaves)

1 tablespoon olive oil

1 medium boiling (waxy) potato, peeled, quartered lengthwise, and thinly sliced

1 scallion, thinly sliced

5 large eggs

½ cup crumbled feta cheese

Pinch salt

Generous seasoning freshly ground black pepper

½ tablespoon butter

1. Wash the spinach and drain it well. Crowd it into an 8- to 10-inch non-stick skillet and cook, covered, over medium heat just until it wilts. Place the spinach in a strainer and press out any liquid with the back of a large spoon. Let it cool.

2. Wipe the skillet clean, and pour in the olive oil. Heat it over medium heat, then add the potato and fry it until tender and golden, about 10 minutes. Stir in the scallion and cook 1 minute. Tip the vegetables onto a plate and let cool.

3. Thoroughly beat the eggs in a medium-size bowl. Stir in the feta cheese, salt, pepper, spinach, and potato mixture.

4. Melt the ½ tablespoon of butter in the skillet over medium-low heat and swirl it around to coat the sides. Pour in the egg mixture. After about 5 minutes when the edges begin to set, help the liquid egg pour over the sides of the frittata by occasionally loosen-

ing the edges with a rubber spatula and tilting the pan. It should take about 15 minutes for the frittata to become almost completely set.

5. Preheat the broiler. When the frittata is about 80 percent cooked, slide it under the broiler for a minute or so until the top is set. (If the handle of your pan isn't ovenproof, wrap a few layers of foil around it before placing the pan under the broiler.) Cut the frittata and place it on plates, but let it cool a little before serving it.

Roasted Vegetable Frittata

Although this recipe technically takes more than 30 minutes of cooking, I count it among my quick meals because it is so easy to prepare. Think of this frittata when you plan a picnic; it is also delicious cold or at room temperature.

Serves 4

1 medium-large boiling (waxy) potato, peeled, quartered, and very thinly sliced

1 red bell pepper, cored and cut into $1/4$-inch-thick strips

1 green bell pepper, cored and cut into $1/4$-inch-thick strips

2 medium-large tomatoes, cored and cut into sixths

1 medium red onion, cut into sixths and sections separated

6 garlic cloves, each halved

Salt

Freshly ground black pepper to taste

$2\frac{1}{2}$ tablespoons olive oil

$1\frac{1}{2}$ teaspoons chopped fresh rosemary, or $1/4$ teaspoon crumbled dried

8 black olives (Kalamata or oil-cured), pitted and halved (page 95)

8 large eggs

$1/2$ cup (3 ounces) finely cubed mozzarella cheese

1. Preheat the oven to 425 degrees. Combine the potato, peppers, tomatoes, red onion, garlic, and salt and pepper to taste in a large bowl. Pour on $1\frac{1}{2}$ tablespoons of the olive oil and toss to coat well. (This mixture can be prepared up to 4 hours in advance.)

2. Spread the vegetables onto a baking sheet and cook 20–30 minutes, or until they are very soft and brown. (You don't want crisp vegetables for this frittata.) Remove from the oven and sprinkle on the rosemary and black olives. Let cool to warm or room temperature.

3. Meanwhile beat the eggs in a large bowl with $1/4$ teaspoon salt. Stir in the mozzarella cheese and then the roasted vegetables.

4. Place the remaining tablespoon of olive oil in a 10-inch non-stick skillet and heat over medium-low heat, tilting the pan to coat the sides with oil. Pour in the egg mixture and cook about 5 minutes. At this point the edges will have begun to set. You can help the liquid egg pour over the sides of the frittata by occasionally running a rubber spatula around the edges of the frittata and tilting the pan. It should take about 15–20 minutes for the frittata to become almost completely set.

5. Preheat the broiler. When the frittata is about 80 percent set, place it under the broiler to finish cooking the top layer. (If the handle of your pan isn't ovenproof, wrap a few layers of foil around it before placing the pan under the broiler.) Cut the frittata into wedges and place on serving plates, but let cool somewhat before serving. It is better when not piping hot.

Broccoli and Smoked Cheese Frittata

Broccoli and smoked cheese animate this simple frittata with their highly compatible flavors. To create a tender frittata that also has a fresh look, you must precook the broccoli to just the right stage—no longer crunchy yet still bright green. Be attentive! Sweet Potato and Red Pepper Home Fries (page 160) would be a tantalizing match with this frittata.

Serves 2

1 tablespoon olive oil

2 garlic cloves, minced

4–5 cups tiny broccoli florets (from about 1 bunch broccoli)

¼ cup water

5 large eggs

¼ teaspoon salt

Generous seasoning freshly ground black pepper

½ cup grated smoked Gouda or mozzarella cheese

½ tablespoon butter

1. Heat the oil in an 8- to 10-inch non-stick skillet over medium heat. Add the garlic and cook 30 seconds. Stir in the broccoli florets and the ¼ cup of water. Cover the pan and cook the broccoli until it is tender but still bright green. Taste one to be sure it is cooked; you don't want crunchy broccoli in this frittata. If the water has not completely evaporated, cook, uncovered, until it evaporates. Place the broccoli on a plate and let cool. Wipe the pan clean.

2. Beat the eggs in a large bowl. Mix in the salt, pepper, smoked cheese, and cooled broccoli.

3. Melt the butter in the skillet over medium-low heat and swirl it around to coat the sides of the pan. Pour in the egg mixture. After about 5 minutes when the edges begin to set, let the liquid egg pour over the sides of the frittata by occasionally loosening the

edges of the frittata with a rubber spatula and tilting the pan. It should take about 15 minutes for the frittata to become almost completely set.

4. Preheat the broiler. When the frittata is about 80 percent set, slide it under the broiler for a minute or so until the top is cooked. (If the handle of your pan isn't oven-proof, wrap a few layers of foil around it before placing the pan under the broiler.) Cut the frittata and place it on serving plates, but let cool a few minutes before serving.

Zucchini, Red Pepper, and Onion Frittata

I cook the onion and red pepper until they are very soft, almost caramelized, because they render a wonderful flavor this way. At first the vegetables will take up a lot of room in the sauté pan, so it is easier to use a large skillet for this step, then switch to a medium-size non-stick pan for the cooking of the frittata.

Serves 2–3

1 tablespoon olive oil
1 medium onion, halved vertically and thinly sliced
1 red bell pepper, cut into very thin strips
1 medium zucchini, quartered lengthwise and very thinly sliced
5 large eggs
3 tablespoons grated Parmesan cheese
¹/₂ cup finely chopped fresh parsley
¹/₄ teaspoon salt
Generous seasoning freshly ground black pepper
¹/₂ tablespoon unsalted butter

1. Heat the oil in a large skillet over medium heat. Add the onion and red pepper and cook, tossing often, for 10 minutes. Cover the pan and cook 10 more minutes, or until the vegetables are soft and beginning to brown. Toss occasionally.

2. Mix in the zucchini and cook until tender yet slightly crisp, about 5 minutes. Remove the pan from the heat.

3. Meanwhile thoroughly beat the eggs in a large bowl. Beat in the Parmesan cheese, parsley, salt, and pepper. If you are going to cook the frittata immediately, then stir in the vegetable mixture; otherwise, let the vegetables cool before mixing them into the eggs.

4. Melt the butter in a 10-inch non-stick skillet over medium-low heat and swirl it around to coat the sides of the pan. Pour in the egg mixture. After about 5 minutes when

the edges begin to set, help the liquid egg pour over the sides of the frittata by occasionally loosening the edges with a rubber spatula and tilting the pan. It should take about 15 minutes for the frittata to become almost completely set.

5. Preheat the broiler. When the frittata is about 80 percent set, slide it under the broiler for a minute or so until the top is cooked. (If the handle of your pan isn't oven-proof, wrap a few layers of foil around it before placing the pan under the broiler.) Cut the frittata and place it on plates, but let it cool a little before serving it.

Shiitake Mushroom and Roasted Red Pepper Omelet

You'll only need about 3 ounces of these fabulous fungi to treat yourself to this savory omelet. The rich flavor and chewy texture of shiitakes make them one of the preeminent mushrooms, so do add them to your repertoire if you haven't done so already.

Serves 2

4 teaspoons olive oil

1 medium onion, halved and thinly sliced

8 medium (3 ounces) shiitake mushrooms, stems discarded, tops wiped clean and thinly sliced

1/4 cup roasted red peppers, store-bought or freshly roasted (page 19), cut into thin strips

1/2 teaspoon minced fresh thyme, or 1/4 teaspoon dried

1/4 cup finely chopped fresh parsley

Salt

Freshly ground black pepper to taste

2 tablespoons sour cream

4 large eggs

2 tablespoons water

1. To make the filling, heat 2 teaspoons of the olive oil in a medium-size skillet over medium heat. Add the onion and sauté until they begin to get tender, about 10 minutes. Stir in the mushrooms and cook until tender and juicy, about 10 more minutes.

2. Mix in the red peppers, thyme, parsley, salt, pepper, and sour cream, and keep hot.

3. Beat the eggs with the water and 1/4 teaspoon salt in a medium-size bowl.

4. Make the omelets one at a time. Heat 1 teaspoon of the oil in an 8-inch, preferably non-stick, skillet over medium-high heat. When the pan is very hot, pour in half of the egg mixture. It should immediately set at the edges. With an inverted spatula push the cooked edges toward the center while tipping the pan to let the liquid egg run out to the hot pan. When very little uncooked egg remains, spoon half of the hot filling onto one side of the omelet. Immediately fold the omelet in half and flip it onto a plate.

Caramelized Onion Omelet

I love to make this omelet when I don't have much on hand for dinner. Little can beat the flavor of caramelized onions, and they are so easy to prepare. Cook the onions slowly (you'll be able to accomplish other tasks during that time), and you'll have an incomparable omelet filling.

Serves 2

4 teaspoons olive oil
2 large onions, halved vertically and thinly sliced
Pinch sugar
4 large eggs
2 tablespoons water
$\frac{1}{4}$ teaspoon salt
Freshly ground black pepper to taste
$\frac{2}{3}$ cup grated sharp Cheddar cheese

1. Heat 2 teaspoons of the oil in a large skillet over medium-low heat. Add the onions and sugar and cook slowly, stirring frequently, until the onions are very soft and a deep caramel color, about 20 minutes. Keep hot over low heat.

2. Beat the eggs with the water, salt, and pepper in a medium-size bowl. Have the cheese ready and near the stove.

3. Make the omelets one at a time for maximum control. Heat 1 teaspoon of the oil over medium-high heat in a medium-size non-stick skillet and swirl it around to coat the sides of the pan. When the pan is very hot, pour in *half* the egg mixture. It should set immediately at the edges. With an inverted spatula push the cooked edges toward the center while tipping the pan to let the uncooked egg run out to the hot pan. When very little liquid egg remains, spoon *half* the onions onto one side of the omelet, then sprinkle on half the cheese. Immediately fold the omelet in half, then flip it onto a plate. This should all take less than one minute. Repeat to make another omelet.

Leek and Ricotta Omelet

Leeks and ricotta cheese both have a natural sweetness and delightfully enhance one another in this toothsome filling.

Serves 2

2 large leeks (to yield 2 ½ cups sliced leeks)
4 teaspoons unsalted butter
Salt
Freshly ground black pepper
¼ cup part-skim ricotta cheese
4 large eggs
2 tablespoons water

1. Cut the root ends off the leeks plus all but 2 inches of the green tops. Slice the leeks in half lengthwise. Under cold running water rinse the leeks, fingering through all the leaves to dislodge any hidden dirt. Do this thoroughly to rid them of *all* their sand. Thinly slice the leeks, discarding any thick, dark green pieces.

2. Heat 2 teaspoons of the butter in a medium-size skillet over medium heat. Add the leeks and sauté until soft and tender, about 10 minutes. Season generously with salt and pepper, then stir in the ricotta cheese. Heat until the ricotta gets hot, then keep the mixture hot over low heat.

3. In a medium-size bowl beat the eggs with ¼ teaspoon of salt and the water.

4. Make the omelets one at a time. Heat 1 teaspoon of the butter in an 8-inch, preferably non-stick, skillet over medium-high heat. When the pan is very hot, pour in half of the egg mixture. It should immediately set at the edges. With an inverted spatula push the cooked edges toward the center while tipping the pan to let the liquid egg run out to the hot pan. When very little uncooked egg remains, spoon half of the hot filling onto one side of the omelet. Immediately fold the omelet in half and flip it onto a plate. Repeat to make one more omelet.

Potato, Pepper, and Tomato Omelet

Here's a mélange of flavors that were meant for each other. I like this filling to be soft, almost jam-like, so I don't aim for crunchy, crisp vegetables here (and neither should you!). If you don't want a spicy dimension, use plain Monterey Jack cheese rather than the one with the jalapeños added. In either case, you'll love this homey omelet.

Serves 2

1 tablespoon plus 2 teaspoons olive oil

1 medium boiling (waxy) potato, peeled, quartered, and thinly sliced

½ green bell pepper, very thinly sliced into 1-inch strips

1 medium onion, quartered and very thinly sliced

2 plum tomatoes, cored, seeded, and finely diced

¼ teaspoon dried oregano

Salt

Freshly ground black pepper

4 large eggs

2 tablespoons water

⅔ cup grated Monterey Jack cheese with jalapeño peppers (see Headnote)

1. Heat the tablespoon of oil in a medium-size, preferably non-stick, skillet over medium heat. Add the potato and cook, tossing often, until tender, about 10 minutes.

2. Add the green pepper and onion and sauté about 5 minutes, then cover the pan and cook 5 more minutes, or until the vegetables are very tender. Add the tomatoes and oregano, season generously with salt and pepper, and cook 5 more minutes, or until the tomatoes are soft and the mixture is somewhat like jam. Keep hot while you prepare the eggs.

3. Beat the eggs with the water and ¼ teaspoon salt. Have the cheese ready and near the stove.

4. Make two omelets, one at a time. Heat 1 teaspoon of the oil in an 8-inch, preferably

non-stick, skillet over medium-high heat. When the pan is very hot, pour in *half* of the egg mixture. It should immediately set at the edges. With an inverted spatula push the cooked edges toward the center while tipping the pan to let the uncooked egg run out to the hot pan. When very little uncooked egg remains, spoon half of the hot filling onto one side of the omelet. Sprinkle on half the cheese. Immediately fold the omelet in half, then flip it onto a plate. Repeat to make one more omelet.

Portobello Mushroom and Caramelized Shallot Omelet

Here is another filling that creates a special meal out of an omelet. Keep the shallots in chunks when you cook them for soft pockets of caramelized shallots in your filling.

Serves 2

6 teaspoons unsalted butter, divided
4 golf-ball-size shallots, each quartered
Pinch sugar
4 portobello mushrooms (3-inch diameter), stems discarded and caps sliced $\frac{1}{4}$ inch thick
Salt
Freshly ground black pepper to taste
$\frac{1}{2}$ teaspoon minced fresh or 1 teaspoon dried tarragon
3 tablespoons soft mild goat cheese
4 large eggs
2 tablespoons water

1. Melt 2 teaspoons butter in a medium-size skillet over medium heat. Add the shallots and sugar and toss. Lower the heat to medium-low and cover the pan. Cook the shallots until they are soft and brown, about 10 minutes. Remove the cover and toss occasionally. Scrape the shallots into a bowl, then wash the pan.

2. Melt 2 teaspoons of the butter over medium heat in the same skillet. Add the mushrooms and sauté until brown and juicy, about 10 minutes. Stir in the shallots, salt, pepper, and tarragon. Gently stir in the goat cheese. Keep the mixture hot.

3. In a medium-size bowl beat the eggs with the water and some salt to taste.

4. Make the omelets one at a time. Heat 1 teaspoon of the oil in an 8-inch non-stick skillet over medium-high heat. When the pan is very hot, pour in *half* of the egg mixture. It should immediately set at the edges. With an inverted spatula push the set egg toward the center and tip the pan to let the liquid run back to the edge. When most of egg is cooked, spoon half of the hot filling onto one side of the omelet. Immediately fold the omelet in half and flip it onto a plate.

Stove-Top Dinners

Tasty combinations of ingredients cooked together in a skillet characterize these wholesome meals. Polenta or couscous may be an accompaniment, or sometimes a stew-like mixture such as White Bean, Sweet Potato, and Pepper Ragout (page 200) can stand on its own. Whatever the case, these hearty dinners are easy to prepare, and most can be made in advance and reheated.

Potato and Vegetable Curry

The flavor and silken consistency of this sauce are unsurpassed. This could be an ideal dish for quick entertaining (it doubles easily), with a spread of side dishes to add to the festiveness: Hot pita bread, chutney, and a cucumber raita (yogurt and grated cucumber salad) are ideal. Take time to cut the vegetables into small pieces to keep the cooking time down to a minimum.

Canned coconut milk is a boon for the quick cook because it is made only of coconut and water (without additives), and is a close second to freshly made coconut milk. Don't worry if it is very thick in the can; it will "melt" when heated.

Serves 2–3

2 tablespoons canola oil

1 onion, minced

3 garlic cloves, minced

1 teaspoon minced fresh gingerroot

2 teaspoons curry powder

1 teaspoon ground cumin

$^{1}/_{4}$ teaspoon ground cardamom

1 cinnamon stick

1 cup seeded and finely diced tomato, fresh or canned

1 (14-ounce) can unsweetened coconut milk

$^{1}/_{2}$ teaspoon salt

2 medium red-skinned potatoes, cut into $^{1}/_{2}$-inch dice (no bigger)

1 large sweet potato or yam, peeled and cut into $^{1}/_{2}$- inch dice

3 cups finely chopped cabbage

1 cup frozen peas, thawed

1. In a large skillet heat the oil over medium heat. Add the onion and cook, stirring often, for 5 minutes. Add the garlic and gingerroot and cook 2 minutes. Stir in the spices and cinnamon stick and "toast" them for 30 seconds, stirring continuously.

2. Stir in the tomato, coconut milk, and salt, and mix well. Mix in the potatoes, sweet potato, and cabbage, and cover the pan. Bring to a boil, then reduce the heat to a simmer. Cook about 20 minutes, or until the potatoes are tender. Stir in the peas and cook 1 more minute, or until the peas are hot throughout. Remove the cinnamon stick before serving.

Note: If you make the curry in advance, don't add the peas until you reheat it. Also, the sauce will thicken when cooled, so you might need to sprinkle in a tablespoon or so of water upon reheating.

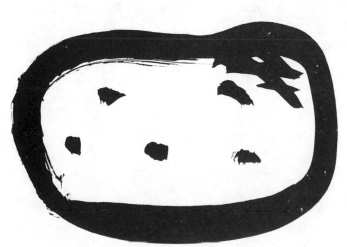

Couscous Topped with White Beans, Tomatoes, and Zucchini

This dish has a tasty and satisfying sauce that captures the flavors of southern France. To make this quickly, I use canned beans. Cannellini (white kidney beans) would be my bean of choice if I were to cook them from scratch; however, canned cannellini are usually overcooked and too soft, so I prefer a small white bean, such as Great Northern or navy beans, when I choose to use canned beans.

Serves 3–4

The Vegetables
2 tablespoons olive oil
1 onion, finely diced
4 garlic cloves, minced
1 medium zucchini, quartered lengthwise and thinly sliced on the diagonal
1 (16-ounce) can tomatoes, finely chopped with their juice
1 (16-ounce) can small white beans, well rinsed and drained
1 tablespoon chopped fresh basil, or $\frac{1}{2}$ teaspoon dried
1 teaspoon chopped fresh rosemary, or $\frac{1}{4}$ teaspoon dried, crumbled
Salt
Generous seasoning freshly ground black pepper

The Couscous
$1\frac{1}{2}$ cups water
$\frac{1}{4}$ teaspoon salt
1 tablespoon unsalted butter
1 cup couscous

1. Heat the oil in a large skillet over medium heat. Add the onion and sauté until tender but not brown, about 10 minutes. Add the garlic and zucchini and cook 5 minutes, or until the zucchini is beginning to get tender but is still crisp.
2. Stir in the tomatoes, beans, herbs, salt, and pepper and cook, tossing occasionally,

until the zucchini is tender and the sauce has thickened slightly, about 5 minutes. (The vegetables may be prepared to this point up to 4 hours in advance and reheated.)

3. Meanwhile cook the couscous. Bring the water, salt, and butter to a boil in a small saucepan. Pour in the couscous, cover the pot, and remove it from the heat. Let sit 5 minutes, fluff with a fork, then cover again and let sit 5 more minutes. Serve a portion on each plate and top with a mound of the vegetable mixture.

Thai Fried Rice

Fried rice requires a little forethought because you have to begin with *cold,* cooked rice to obtain fluffy results, but it's worth the effort when you are in the mood for a grain-based dish that's teeming with flavor. This recipe benefits from reheating, so don't hesitate to make the entire dish in advance and reheat it over low heat or in the oven. Cold, leftover fried rice is delicious as a salad; if you need to pack a lunch for work, take a container of this rice.

Serves 4 as a main course

1 teaspoon plus 1 tablespoon canola oil

2 eggs, well beaten

1 red bell pepper, cut into small dice

1 teaspoon minced gingerroot

2 garlic cloves, minced

1/4 teaspoon crushed red pepper flakes

3 scallions, thinly sliced

6 cups cold cooked brown rice (made from 2 cups raw rice boiled with 5 1/2 cups water)

1/4 cup tamari soy sauce

1 tablespoon tomato paste

1 tablespoon lime juice

2 tablespoons oriental sesame oil

2 cups bean sprouts

1 tablespoon minced fresh basil, or 1/2 teaspoon dried

1 tablespoon minced fresh mint, or 1 teaspoon dried

1. To make shredded egg for the rice, heat the teaspoon of oil in a small skillet over medium-high heat. Pour in the eggs and scramble a bit with a fork. Let the eggs cook into a "pancake," then flip over and cook on the other side. This should all take about 1 minute. Place the pancake on a plate and let cool slightly. Cut the pancake into small strips and set aside.

2. Heat the remaining tablespoon of oil in a large, preferably non-stick, skillet over medium heat. Add the bell pepper and sauté 3 minutes. Stir in the ginger, garlic, and red pepper flakes and cook 2 minutes, tossing often. Stir in the scallions and cook 30 seconds.

3. Break up the cold rice if it is clumpy, then mix it into the vegetable mixture.

4. In a small bowl mix together the soy sauce, tomato paste, lime juice, and sesame oil. Pour over the rice and toss gently to coat with the sauce.

5. Stir in the bean sprouts, basil, mint, and shredded egg. Heat until hot throughout, about 3 minutes. Serve immediately, or cool and reheat it within 2 days.

Polenta with Broccoli and Garlic

Few vegetables can compete with broccoli from a nutritional standpoint, and I think the same is true regarding flavor. The fact that it is commonplace doesn't diminish its appeal. Bolstered by garlic and hot pepper flakes, it's a delicious match for this cheesy polenta.

Serves 3–4

The Polenta

4 cups light vegetable stock, store-bought or homemade (page 13)

¼ teaspoon salt

1¼ cups cornmeal

⅓ cup grated Parmesan cheese

2 tablespoons unsalted butter, cut into bits

The Vegetables

2 tablespoons olive oil

6 garlic cloves, minced

¼ teaspoon crushed red pepper flakes

1 large bunch broccoli, cut into tiny florets, stalks peeled and diced (5–6 cups total)

⅓ cup water

3 plum tomatoes, seeded and finely diced

Salt

1. To make the polenta, bring the vegetable stock and salt to a boil in a medium-size, heavy-bottomed saucepan. Meanwhile prepare all the ingredients for this dish and set them out in front of you.

2. When the stock boils, reduce the heat to low and very slowly drizzle in the cornmeal, whisking constantly with a wire whisk. Continue to cook the polenta, whisking continuously, until it is thick like mashed potatoes and begins to tear away from the sides of the pot, about 5 minutes. Whisk in the cheese and butter, cover the pot, then remove it

from the heat. The polenta can be kept like this for 10 minutes or so.

3. Heat the oil in a large skillet over medium heat. Add the garlic and red pepper flakes and cook 1 minute. Mix in the broccoli, toss well, then pour in the water. Cover the pan and cook the broccoli until tender, about 5 minutes. Remove the cover and stir in the tomatoes and salt to taste. Cook, uncovered, for about 2 minutes, or until the tomatoes are soft and most of the liquid has evaporated.

4. To serve, spoon a mound of polenta on each dinner plate. Top with the broccoli mixture.

Gorgonzola Polenta with Spinach and Exotic Mushrooms

If you don't have access to assorted, exotic mushrooms (technically they are no longer "wild," since they are cultivated), common white button mushrooms will also be delicious here, lending their juices and buttery flavor.

You can make the sautéed vegetables a bit in advance and quickly reheat them; however, the polenta should be prepared at the last minute.

Serves 4

3 $^1/_2$ cups water

2 tablespoons olive oil

6 garlic cloves, minced

$^1/_4$ teaspoon crushed red pepper flakes

$^3/_4$ pound assorted exotic and common mushrooms (such as shiitake, oyster, cremini, and white button), wiped clean and sliced (about 4 $^1/_2$ cups sliced)

1 (1-pound) bunch fresh spinach, or 1 (10-ounce) bag fresh spinach, stems discarded and leaves washed

Salt to taste

The Polenta

$^1/_4$ teaspoon salt

1 $^1/_4$ cups cornmeal

1 tablespoon unsalted butter

2 tablespoons grated Parmesan cheese

3 ounces Gorgonzola or other blue cheese, finely diced (about $^3/_4$ cup diced)

1. Bring the water to a boil in a medium-size, heavy-bottomed saucepan.

2. Meanwhile heat the oil in a large skillet over medium-high heat. Add the garlic and red pepper flakes and cook 30 seconds. Immediately drop in the mushrooms and toss well. Cook, tossing often, until the mushrooms render their juices and begin to brown.

3. Pile on the spinach, toss, then cover the pan. Cook just until the spinach wilts, about

3 minutes. Remove the cover, then season with salt to taste. Keep the vegetables warm while you make the polenta. (The vegetables may be prepared to this point up to 4 hours in advance and reheated.)

4. When the water boils, add the $\frac{1}{4}$ teaspoon salt, then reduce the heat to medium-low. Very slowly drizzle in the cornmeal, whisking all the while with a wire whisk. Cook the polenta about 5 minutes, or until it pulls away from the sides of the pan. Keep whisking often while it cooks to keep it smooth.

5. Drop in the butter, Parmesan cheese, and Gorgonzola and stir just until blended.

6. Spoon some polenta onto each serving plate, then top with some of the vegetable mixture and its juices.

Polenta with
Spicy Tomato-Garlic Sauce

Such a simple topping but with so much punch! This is bound to become one of your favorites.

Serves 3–4

The Sauce

2 tablespoons olive oil

8 garlic cloves, coarsely chopped (no less!)

$^1\!/_4$ teaspoon crushed red pepper flakes

1 (28-ounce) can imported plum tomatoes, drained and very finely diced

2 tablespoons mixed chopped fresh herbs (such as basil, rosemary, and parsley), or 1 teaspoon
   dried

$^1\!/_4$ teaspoon salt

Pinch sugar

Freshly ground black pepper to taste

The Polenta

$3^1\!/_2$ cups water

$^1\!/_4$ teaspoon salt

1 cup cornmeal

1 tablespoon unsalted butter

$^1\!/_4$ cup grated Parmesan cheese

$^1\!/_2$ cup grated cheese (such as mozzarella, Fontina, Monterey Jack, or Muenster)

1. To make the sauce, heat the oil in a medium-size skillet over medium heat. Add the garlic and pepper flakes and cook 1 minute.

2. Stir in the tomatoes, herbs, salt, sugar, and pepper. Simmer just until the juices thicken, about 10 minutes. (The sauce may be prepared to this point up to 4 hours in advance. Reheat and keep warm while making the polenta.)

3. To make the polenta, bring the water and salt to a boil in a $2^1\!/_2$- to 3-quart heavy-

bottomed saucepan. Reduce the heat to a simmer, then very slowly drizzle in the corn-meal, whisking all the while with a wire whisk. Whisk continuously until the polenta is the consistency of mashed potatoes and begins to tear away from the sides of the pan, about 5 minutes. Whisk in the butter and both cheeses. (At this point you can cover the polenta, turn off the heat, and keep it hot for up to 10 minutes before serving.)

4. Pour some polenta on each dinner plate, then spoon some sauce on the center of the polenta. Serve immediately.

White Bean, Sweet Potato, and Pepper Ragout

The great marriage of colors and flavors in this peasant-style mélange calls for some crusty French or Italian bread to wipe up the tantalizing juices that will accumulate on your plate.

Serves 2–3

2 tablespoons olive oil

1 red bell pepper, cut into strips 2 × ½ inch

1 green bell pepper, cut into strips 2 × ½ inch

1 large sweet potato or yam, peeled, cut in half lengthwise, and sliced ¼ inch thick

4 garlic cloves, minced

½ teaspoon finely chopped fresh rosemary, or ¼ teaspoon dried, crumbled

1 (14-ounce) can diced tomatoes with their juice

2 cups freshly cooked or canned small white beans, well rinsed and drained if canned

¼ cup water

Salt and generous seasoning freshly ground black pepper

1. Heat the oil in a large skillet over medium heat. Add the red and green peppers and sauté 5 minutes, tossing frequently. The peppers should begin to get tender.

2. Stir in the sweet potato, garlic, and rosemary, and cook, stirring often, for 10 minutes. The mixture will begin to brown and bits of it will stick to the pan—this is good, for the scrapings will later be incorporated into the sauce and add flavor.

3. Mix in the tomatoes, white beans, water, salt, and pepper. Cover the pan and simmer everything for about 15 minutes, or until the sweet potatoes are tender. Periodically remove the cover and scrape the bottom of the skillet to loosen those tasty bits that have stuck to the pan. There should be some thickened juices remaining when the dish is ready to be served. If it seems dry, add a bit more water and cook a few minutes until thickened. (The ragout may be prepared to this point up to 4 hours in advance and reheated.) Serve on dinner plates or in shallow pasta bowls with some bread alongside it.

White Beans with Spinach, Garlic, and Tomatoes

There is a recent enthusiasm for most things Mediterranean. And with good reason. These stewed white beans are an example of the simplicity and quality that one finds in rustic dishes of the Italian home cook. Garlic permeates the thick sauce that is created, which of course makes you want to clean your plate with some crusty Tuscan-style bread.

I have had good results making these stewed beans with canned small white beans (find a brand that offers firm, not mushy, beans), so don't hesitate to make this dish if you are pressed for time.

Serves 4

¼ cup fruity olive oil

6 garlic cloves, minced

3 plum tomatoes, seeded and diced

6 cups freshly cooked or canned small white beans, well rinsed and drained if canned

⅓ cup vegetable stock, store-bought or homemade (page 13)

5 cups torn spinach leaves (torn into small pieces)

Generous seasoning freshly ground black pepper

1. Heat the oil in a large skillet over medium heat. Add the garlic and cook 30 seconds. Stir in the tomatoes and sauté, tossing often, until the tomatoes are soft, about 7 minutes.

2. Stir in the beans and stock and bring to a simmer. Pile on the spinach, cover the pan, and cook just until wilted, about 3 minutes. Season generously with pepper. When done, the mixture should have thickened, sauce-like juices, not watery, not dry. If it's too soupy, cook a few minutes more; if too dry, add a bit more stock. Serve on flat dinner plates or in large, shallow pasta bowls with a good chunk of bread on the side.

Tofu and Tempeh Favorites

Tofu

Tofu, also called soybean curd, is made in a similar way as cheese. Soybeans are cooked and mashed, then their liquid is pressed out of them. This soy milk is mixed with a coagulant to cause the curds to separate from the whey. The curds are then pressed into cakes to form tofu. Tofu is an excellent source of protein and iron and a good source of calcium. It is widely used throughout China and Japan.

I buy tofu in sealed packages rather than out of open bins because tofu can be a haven for bacteria when it is exposed to dust and dirt in a store. Once the package of tofu is opened and a portion remains to be stored, place it in some fresh water in a covered container in the refrigerator.

Change the water daily until you use the tofu. Spoiled tofu will have a slimy feel to it, take on a yellowish tinge, and taste sour.

Cooking with Tofu

Have you ever wondered why tofu can be so appealing at times (like in Chinese restaurants), and at other times be off-putting? It's all in the texture; it will make or break a tofu dish.

When tofu is cooked *properly,* that is, fried or roasted so that it is golden all over, it retains a chewy consistency. If this tofu is then cooled, as in Marinated Fried Tofu and Vegetable Salad with Mesclun (page 206), Bow-Tie Pasta and Fried Tofu Salad with Sesame Dressing (page 210), Mock Chicken Salad (page 212), and Roasted Marinated Tofu (page 214), the tofu becomes even firmer and more palatable. Although tofu aficionados enjoy tofu fixed many different ways—even uncooked—I have found that a crisply cooked treatment is the best way to introduce tofu to newcomers. If you spot a tofu recipe (in another cookbook) that calls for stir-frying a few ingredients and then adding the tofu—beware! The tofu will not become sufficiently crispy if other ingredients in the pan give off moisture, etc. Soft, wobbly tofu has turned off many an eager novice.

I always use extra-firm tofu because I want it to retain its shape when I cook it, and I prefer its texture. Even in salad dressings that require pureeing I use the extra-firm variety because it will become creamy, and this allows me to purchase one variety of tofu for all purposes.

Tofu and other soy products have gotten a lot of attention recently because Asian women who consume ample amounts of these foods have been found to have noticeably lower mortality rates from breast cancer, and significantly weaker menopausal symptoms, such as hot flashes and night sweats. Soy is a plant source of phytoestrogens, which help compensate women for natural estrogen losses.

So if you not only want to increase your tofu consumption but also *enjoy* eating it, try it in the following recipes and you'll see that tofu doesn't deserve to be the brunt of all those food jokes, unless, of course, it gets improperly cooked—as in those *other* cookbooks!

Pan-Frying and Roasting Tofu

In order to pan-fry (cook in a skillet with a minimal amount of oil) or roast (bake in the oven at high heat) tofu properly, that is, create a crisp, uniformly golden exterior, you must begin with dry tofu. Oil and water don't mix, and the moisture from the tofu will interfere with the oil's ability to brown the tofu.

You can "dry" tofu a number of ways. Here are two: I have found that the easiest and quickest way to rid tofu of its excess moisture is to cut it into slices, lay them on one half of a cotton or linen kitchen towel, then fold over the other half of the towel to cover the tofu. Now gently press on the tofu to release its moisture into the towel. You can also use paper towels to pat the tofu dry. Repeat this "patting" a few times until the tofu no longer feels wet—just moist. Cut the tofu into cubes (or whatever shape the recipe calls for), and pat them dry once again. This might sound like a lot of patting, but it is actually quite quick and hassle-free. Wash the towel(s) you used, and keep them available for this and other kitchen tasks.

The other method of draining tofu is to place the tofu on a dinner plate. Put a salad-size plate on top of the tofu, and weigh it down with a heavy can (such as a 32-ounce can of tomatoes). Place a teaspoon under one end of the dinner plate to slightly tilt it; this will drain the released liquid to one end of the plate. Pour off the liquid as it accumulates. It will take about an hour to thoroughly drain the tofu. After you cut the tofu into slices or cubes, you will still have to pat them dry, but because you are starting with a drier tofu than in the first method, you won't have to pat them as much.

Now you are ready to fry or roast the tofu. If you use a non-stick skillet for pan-frying, you'll be amazed at how easily you can achieve a golden crust on the tofu. If your skillet isn't a non-stick pan, you'll have to toss the tofu frequently to prevent it from sticking. In either case, heat the amount of oil specified in the recipe until it is very hot but not yet smoking. You don't want to add tofu to warm oil. Keep the pan hot and fry the tofu until it is evenly golden all over. To roast tofu properly (see Roasted Marinated Tofu, page 214), make sure your oven is sufficiently preheated, and use a heavy ceramic or Corning Ware baking dish. A roasting pan might cause the tofu to stick. Both methods of cooking tofu will produce wonderful results.

Marinated Fried Tofu and Vegetable Salad with Mesclun

Cold, fried tofu, as in this very special salad, is the best way to introduce tofu to a hesitant newcomer. By frying the tofu first, it gets crispy and chewy, and then absorbs the garlicky marinade, making it resemble chicken in flavor and texture. (Lest it sound odd to you that I would mention chicken in a vegetarian cookbook, I should explain that although I've been a vegetarian for nearly 30 years, I never said that chicken doesn't taste good!)

Using fried tofu rather than raw tofu in a salad was a revelation to me. I've always loved the way tofu is transformed when it is cooked in a little oil, but until recently I never thought it would be good cold. Now I can't get enough of it.

A non-stick skillet makes frying tofu infinitely easier than when cooked in other pans because moist tofu tends to stick when fried. If you don't have such a pan, use the heaviest skillet you have and make sure the tofu is patted *very dry* before frying.

Serves 3–4

1 tablespoon canola oil

1 pound extra-firm tofu, cut into ½-inch cubes and patted *very dry*

The Dressing

3 tablespoons lemon juice

2 large garlic cloves, minced

1 teaspoon tamari soy sauce

½ teaspoon salt

Generous seasoning freshly ground black pepper

¼ cup olive oil

4–5 cups tiny broccoli florets

2 large scallions, very thinly sliced

1 red bell pepper, cut into ¾-inch dice

4 cups mesclun (baby salad greens), washed and spun dry

1. Heat the oil in a large, preferably non-stick, skillet over high heat until it is very hot but not smoking. Add the tofu and spread it out so that it is in one layer. Fry it, shaking the pan often to prevent sticking, until it is a rich golden color all over. With a spatula flip it over occasionally so it gets evenly browned. Place it in a large bowl. Set the skillet aside.

2. Combine all the ingredients for the dressing in a jar with a tight-fitting lid and shake vigorously. Pour half the dressing on the hot tofu and toss well. Chill the tofu until it is very cold, about 2 hours.

3. Meanwhile place the broccoli in the skillet, add a little water, and cover the pan. Cook it until it is crisp yet tender, about 4 minutes. Immerse it in a bowl of cold water to stop any further cooking. Drain the broccoli thoroughly, then place it on a cotton or linen kitchen towel and pat it dry.

4. Mix the broccoli, scallions, red pepper, and remaining dressing into the cold tofu. Toss well. Let sit at least 30 minutes to marinate, or chill up to 4 hours then bring close to room temperature so it's cool, not cold.

5. Just before serving, mix in the mesclun. Serve on large plates.

Soba and Fried Tofu Salad
with Shredded Spinach

This salad contains a perfectly harmonious blending of ingredients that seem made for each other. Don't hesitate to make it 1–2 days before you intend to serve it because it will be just as good as the day it was made. Hold off mixing in the spinach, though, until serving time.

I grate the ginger for this salad because I prefer the thin strands. All you have to do is use a knife to scrape the skin off the gingerroot, then grate it on the *coarse* side of the grater (it clogs the finer side). If the pieces are a bit too big, use a large knife to mince them.

A note about soba—try to find a store that sells soba loosely by the pound, instead of in packages. It is considerably cheaper when purchased in bulk. In our town the natural foods store and our upscale marketplace sell them this way.

Serves 4 as a main course

1 pound extra-firm tofu
1 tablespoon canola oil
1 tablespoon tamari soy sauce
1 pound soba (buckwheat noodles)

The Dressing
3 tablespoons tamari soy sauce
3 tablespoons oriental sesame oil
2 tablespoons brown sugar
1 teaspoon hot chili oil
1 tablespoon rice vinegar or red wine vinegar
2 teaspoons scraped then coarsely grated gingerroot

1 tablespoon sesame seeds
2 large scallions, very thinly sliced
4 cups spinach leaves, washed, then stacked and julienned

1. Cut the tofu into ¼-inch-thick slices and pat them *very* dry with a kitchen towel or paper towels. Cut each slice into 4 triangles by cutting a big "X" from corner to corner.

2. Heat the oil in a large, preferably non-stick, skillet over high heat. Add half of the tofu triangles and fry them on both sides until golden brown. Keep the heat high. Remove the tofu and place it in a large bowl. Repeat with the remaining tofu. Pour the tablespoon of tamari on the tofu, toss well, then chill it until it is very cold, about 1½ hours.

3. Meanwhile bring a large stockpot of water to a boil. Drop in the soba and cook until al dente, about 7 minutes. You must watch soba carefully because if it is overcooked it will fall apart, yet you don't want it too firm either. Keep tasting a strand to be certain it is cooked properly. Drain the soba in a colander, then rinse under cold running water. Vigorously shake out all the water, then place the noodles in a large bowl. (Once the noodles are rinsed, they become firmer. Don't worry, though, they will get tender again once they marinate.)

4. Make the dressing by combining all the ingredients in a bowl. Set it aside.

5. Toast the sesame seeds by placing them in a small pot over medium heat. Swirl the pan around until the seeds become fragrant and start to smoke, about 4 minutes. Do not take your eyes off them. When lightly golden, pour them into a small bowl and let them cool.

6. When the tofu is cold, mix it into the noodles along with the sesame seeds and scallions. Pour on the dressing and toss well. Marinate the salad at least 1 hour or up to 2 days before serving. Cover and chill it if it is longer than 2 hours. It is best served cool or at room temperature, so remove it from the refrigerator a half hour or so before serving time. Just before serving, mix in the spinach.

Bow-Tie Pasta and Fried Tofu Salad with Sesame Dressing

Tofu again resembles chicken in this savory marinated pasta salad with Sesame-Ginger Dressing. Farfalle (bow-tie noodles) are especially good here and worth making a special trip for because their delightful shape pairs well with the tofu chunks. This is a great salad for picnics, potlucks, and traveling lunches.

Serves 4 as a main course

Sesame-Ginger Dressing
2 tablespoons tamari soy sauce
2 tablespoons red wine vinegar
1 tablespoon brown sugar
1 large garlic clove, put through a press or minced
1 teaspoon minced gingerroot
1/4 teaspoon salt
Freshly ground black pepper
2 tablespoons oriental sesame oil
1/4 cup canola oil

1 tablespoon canola oil
1 pound extra-firm tofu, cut into 1/2-inch cubes and patted *very* dry
1 pound farfalle (bow-tie pasta)
4 large scallions, very thinly sliced

1. To make the dressing, combine all its ingredients in a jar with a tight-fitting lid and shake vigorously. Set aside.

2. Bring a large stockpot of water to a boil for the pasta. Meanwhile cook the tofu. Place the tablespoon of canola oil in a large, preferably non-stick, skillet and heat the pan over high heat until very hot but not smoking. Add the tofu and let sit in one layer. Shaking the pan to prevent the tofu from sticking, cook the tofu until it is golden underneath,

then with a spatula, toss it around until it is a deep golden color all over. Drop the tofu into a deep, large bowl.

3. Pour about one quarter of the dressing on the tofu and toss well. Let cool.

4. Drop the farfalle into the boiling water and cook until al dente, about 12 minutes. Drain in a colander, then rinse under cold running water. Drain again thoroughly.

5. Mix the farfalle into the tofu. Pour on the remaining dressing and toss well. Sprinkle on the scallions and toss again. Chill the salad at least 2 hours before serving. Serve at room temperature or slightly cool, but not cold.

Mock Chicken Salad

When small bits of cold, fried, chewy tofu get mixed with celery and mayonnaise, a tantalizing sandwich spread is created that is remarkably like chicken salad in flavor and texture. Fried tempeh makes a similar mock chicken salad but has a stronger flavor. Try it with leaf lettuce on a good-quality whole grain bread.

For 4–5 sandwiches

1 pound extra-firm tofu
1 tablespoon canola oil
1 tablespoon tamari soy sauce
1 large scallion, very thinly sliced
1 medium celery rib, very thinly sliced
3 tablespoons mayonnaise
Freshly ground black pepper to taste

1. Place the tofu in a cotton or linen kitchen towel and gather up the sides of the towel to create a pouch of tofu. Twist the ball of tofu until a lot of liquid is released. Drop the tofu ball onto a cutting board, then with a large knife, finely chop it so the pieces are the size of small peas.

2. Heat the oil in a large, non-stick skillet over high heat until it is very hot but not yet smoking. Add the tofu and shake the pan to prevent it from sticking, then, using a spatula, flip it around until it gets evenly golden brown. This should take at least 10 minutes. Keep the heat high. The pan might start to smoke but that's okay; just keep flipping the tofu. When done, drop it into a medium-size bowl and drizzle the soy sauce all over it. Toss well. Let cool 10 minutes, then refrigerate it until very cold, at least 1 hour.

3. Stir in the remaining ingredients. Keep covered and chilled until ready to use.

Curried Tofu "Eggless" Salad

I have a basic version of this sandwich spread in *Quick Vegetarian Pleasures* and I am so fond of it that creating an equally delicious variation seemed an inevitable challenge. The crunchy vegetables, mild spiciness of the curry, and contrasting sweetness of the raisins make this rendition a tough competitor.

For 4 sandwiches

1/2 pound extra-firm tofu

3 tablespoons mayonnaise

3/4 teaspoon curry powder

1 celery rib, very finely diced

1 small carrot, grated

1 1/2 tablespoons raisins

1 scallion, very thinly sliced

1/4 teaspoon salt

Generous seasoning freshly ground black pepper

1. To rid it of excess moisture, place the block of tofu on a linen or cotton kitchen towel and gather up the sides of the towel. Twist the ball of tofu over the sink, letting the released liquid drip into the sink. Open up the towel and drop the tofu into a medium-size bowl. Mash it with a fork until its texture is fine, that is, resembling coarse bread crumbs.

2. Stir in all the remaining ingredients. Cover and chill at least 1 hour so that the flavors can develop. Use as a sandwich spread. It is particularly delicious on toasted bread.

Roasted Marinated Tofu

Here is a treatment of tofu that is an alternative to pan-frying and also produces fabulous results. I love to chill this tofu and add it to salads or just eat it alone. Packed in a plastic container, it makes the perfect portable lunch.

Serves 2–4

1 pound extra-firm tofu
1½ tablespoons tamari soy sauce
1 tablespoon oriental sesame oil
1 teaspoon canola oil
1 tablespoon dry sherry

1. Slice the tofu into ½-inch-thick slices. Lay them on a clean cotton kitchen towel or on paper towels and pat *very* dry. Cut the tofu into cubes, triangles, or any shape of your choice.

2. Combine the soy sauce, sesame oil, canola oil, and sherry in a large bowl. Add the tofu, and very gently toss it with the marinade. Let marinate at least 30 minutes, or cover and chill up to 24 hours.

3. Preheat the oven to 450 degrees. Place the tofu, and its marinade in a single layer in a large, shallow baking dish. Bake 25–30 minutes, or until golden all over. Shake the pan after 15 minutes to prevent the tofu from sticking. Serve warm, or, better yet, cool the tofu, then refrigerate until very cold, at least 2 hours.

Baked Thai-Style Tofu

This method of baking marinated tofu gives it a crispy coating and intensifies all the flavors in the "sauce." You'll also love the ease with which this dish can be put together. A side portion of rice, plain couscous, or Couscous Pilaf with Pistachio Nuts and Scallions (page 164) is the best accompaniment.

Don't hesitate to serve this dynamic tofu dish cold; it would make a great lunch to take to work.

Serves 3

The Marinade

2 tablespoons tamari soy sauce

1 tablespoon oriental sesame oil

1 tablespoon canola oil

$^1/_2$ teaspoon minced gingerroot

1 garlic clove, minced

$^1/_4$ teaspoon crushed red pepper flakes

1 pound extra-firm tofu, cut into $^3/_4$-inch cubes and patted *very* dry

1 red bell pepper, cut into thin strips, $^1/_4 \times 2$ inches

The Sauce

1 tablespoon natural-style peanut butter

2 tablespoons lime juice

1 scallion, very thinly sliced

2 teaspoons finely chopped fresh basil, or $^1/_4$ teaspoon dried

2 teaspoons finely chopped fresh mint, or $^1/_2$ teaspoon dried

1. Combine the marinade ingredients in a large bowl. Using a rubber spatula, gently fold in the tofu and red pepper to coat them evenly with the marinade. Let sit 30 minutes at room temperature, or up to 8 hours chilled. Toss occasionally.

2. Preheat the oven to 450 degrees. Place the tofu mixture and any remaining marinade in a large shallow baking dish so that the tofu rests in one layer. Bake 15 minutes, tossing once with a spatula after about 7 minutes.

3. Meanwhile make the sauce by stirring all its ingredients together with a fork. Remove the tofu from the oven. Spoon on the sauce, then, using a spatula, toss the ingredients together until everything is well coated. Return the dish to the oven and bake undisturbed for 10 minutes. Let the tofu sit at least 10 minutes before serving it, for it is better when warm, not piping hot.

Baked Tofu and Mushrooms Hoisin

Serves 3

The Marinade

2 tablespoons tamari soy sauce

1 tablespoon oriental sesame oil

1 tablespoon vegetable oil

$^1/_2$ teaspoon minced gingerroot

2 garlic cloves, minced

1 pound extra-firm tofu, cut into $^3/_4$-inch cubes and patted *very* dry

$^1/_2$ pound mushrooms, each quartered, large ones cut into sixths

The Sauce

1 $^1/_2$ teaspoons tamari soy sauce

1 tablespoon natural-style peanut butter, smooth or chunky

1 tablespoon hoisin sauce

1 tablespoon dry sherry

1 scallion, very thinly sliced

1. Combine the marinade ingredients in a large bowl. Add the tofu and mushrooms and, using a rubber spatula, gently toss to coat evenly. Let sit 30 minutes, or up to 8 hours, tossing occasionally. If marinating longer than 8 hours, cover and chill. Bring to room temperature before cooking.

2. Preheat the oven to 425 degrees. Combine all of the sauce ingredients—except the scallion—in a small bowl.

3. Place the tofu mixture and its marinade in a shallow baking dish so that it all rests in one layer. Bake 15 minutes, tossing once with a spatula.

4. Remove the dish from the oven, then pour the sauce over the tofu mixture. Toss gently, then sprinkle on the scallion. Return the dish to the oven and bake 10 more minutes. Let sit 10–15 minutes before serving. It should be served warm, not hot.

Penne with Fried Tofu, Roasted Peppers, and Olives

Here's another great way to introduce newcomers to the charm of fried tofu, although in this case the tofu is hot and therefore slightly softer, but still delicious. The Mediterranean flavors of peppers, olives, and basil are an enticing backdrop to these chunks of crispy, fried tofu, which soak up the garlicky sauce and lend this hearty dish some bulk and character.

Serves 4

1 tablespoon canola oil

1 pound extra-firm tofu, cut into ½-inch cubes and patted *very* dry

1 tablespoon tamari soy sauce

1 pound penne

3 tablespoons olive oil

6 garlic cloves, minced

1 (7-ounce jar) roasted red peppers, drained and cut into ½-inch dice (1 cup diced)

10 black olives (your favorite kind), pitted and halved (see page 95)

½ cup chopped fresh parsley

¼ cup chopped fresh basil

½ teaspoon salt

Generous seasoning freshly ground black pepper

¼ cup grated Parmesan cheese

1. Fill a large pot with water and bring to a boil.

2. Heat the oil in a large, preferably non-stick, skillet over high heat until it is very hot but not smoking. Add the tofu and, making sure it is in one layer and not overcrowded, fry it until golden brown all over. Shake the pan to keep it from sticking, and with a spatula flip the tofu around occasionally so it cooks evenly. Drop the tofu into a large bowl, then drizzle on the soy sauce. Toss well. Set the tofu aside.

3. Drop the penne into the boiling water and cook until al dente. Do not overcook it.

4. Meanwhile make the sauce. Heat the olive oil in a large skillet over medium heat. Add the garlic and cook 30 seconds. Do not let it get at all brown. Add the peppers and cook 2 minutes. Stir in the olives, parsley, basil, salt, pepper, and tofu. Toss well. Remove 1/2 cup of the starchy pasta water and stir it into the sauce. Cook 1 minute.

5. Drain the penne in a colander and shake to remove all the water. Return it to the pot or place it in a large bowl. Pour on the sauce and mix well. Sprinkle on the Parmesan cheese, toss, and serve.

Tempeh

Indonesian in origin, tempeh is a fermented soybean product that is made from chopped soybeans mixed with a rhizopus culture which are then pressed together to form a cake. In this state it is considered raw, and it must be cooked before being eaten. Because tempeh has a strong flavor, it doesn't depend on potent seasonings the way tofu does.

High in protein and a good source of iron, tempeh also contains vitamin B_{12}, the one vitamin vegans can have difficulty getting enough of.

Tempeh is sold in tightly sealed packages that display an expiration date. Unlike tofu, it can easily be frozen by just placing the package in the freezer. Fresh tempeh often has black spots on it. These are not a sign of decay, but rather spores of the culture that was mixed with the soybeans. Spoiled tempeh is unmistakable—it will smell foul, feel slimy, and have pink or yellow mold on it.

Cooking with tempeh is easy. It doesn't require any special handling—just chop it into small pieces and sauté them in a skillet until hot throughout.

Barbecued Tempeh Spread

Many people feel that the texture and flavor of tempeh spread are reminiscent of chicken salad. Mixed with this spicy barbecue dressing, it makes a delicious and satisfying sandwich filling that is packed with protein.

Enough for 3–4 sandwiches

1 tablespoon vegetable oil
1½ teaspoons chili powder
8 ounces tempeh, finely chopped
1 celery rib, finely diced
¼ cup minced red onion
¼ cup mayonnaise
2 tablespoons ketchup
½ teaspoon red wine vinegar
1 teaspoon Dijon-style mustard
1 teaspoon molasses
1 small garlic clove, put through a press or minced
Salt
Freshly ground black pepper to taste

1. Heat the oil in a medium-size, preferably non-stick, skillet over medium heat. Stir in the chili powder and cook 10 seconds, then stir in the tempeh and toss to coat it with the chili powder. Cook, tossing frequently, until the tempeh is golden, about 7 minutes.
2. Scrape the tempeh into a bowl and let cool. Stir in the celery and onion.
3. In a small bowl combine all the remaining ingredients. Pour it over the tempeh mixture and toss well. Cover and chill at least 30 minutes, or up to 3 days. Serve as a sandwich spread.

Garlicky Tempeh and Potato Ragout

Tender chunks of tempeh and potatoes simmer in an aromatic, garlic-spiked tomato sauce to make a hearty, one-dish meal that is dairy-free. I prefer red-skinned potatoes in this case because they hold together so well when cooked. A salad and some crusty bread would nicely round out the meal.

Serves 2–3

2 large red-skinned potatoes, cut into small (½-inch) dice

3 tablespoons olive oil

6 garlic cloves, minced

¼ teaspoon crushed red pepper flakes

1 (8-ounce) package tempeh, cut into ½-inch dice

1 (16-ounce) can tomatoes, finely diced with their juice

½ teaspoon salt

Freshly ground black pepper to taste

¼ cup water

¼ cup finely chopped fresh parsley

1. Place the potatoes in a large skillet and add about ½ inch of water. Cover the pan and cook the potatoes over medium heat until tender when gently pierced with a knife, about 7 minutes. Drain the potatoes in a colander and let them sit while proceeding with the next step.

2. Wipe the skillet clean. Pour the oil in the skillet and heat it over medium heat. Add the garlic and red pepper flakes and cook 30 seconds. Stir in the tempeh, toss, and cook 1 minute.

3. Mix in the tomatoes, salt, pepper, and ¼ cup of water. Cover the pan and simmer 5 minutes. Remove the cover and check the thickness of the sauce. If it seems watery, cook a few more minutes uncovered. Just before serving, stir in the parsley.

Pasta and Noodles

No cuisine has helped vegetarian meal planning more than Italy's, most especially with its contribution of pasta. Everyone loves pasta, and its popularity shows no sign of abating.

But what is it that makes some pasta preparations spectacular and others undistinguished? Though plain buttered or oiled noodles can be satisfying, it's really the sauce that makes the dish. It needn't be complex to be delicious; sometimes just a few ingredients like olive oil, garlic, and hot peppers can create a humble yet seductive dressing for pasta. The ingredients must, above all, be intensely flavorful to bring pasta to life. This is equally true of Asian noodles, which are also a fantastic contribution to the vegetarian's repertoire.

The quantity of sauce is another important factor in its ability to enhance pasta. There is a limit to how much we can cut back on fat without destroying our final creation. For a pound of dried pasta, a minimum of $1/4$ cup of olive oil is required to adequately coat the noodles. We can extend our sauce using a tried-and-true trick—adding some starchy pasta water to it—but the $1/4$ cup minimum of olive oil still stands.

Although the importance of a zesty sauce cannot be overemphasized, the *texture* of the pasta is equally significant in producing a superlative pasta dish. If you overcook pasta, no sauce can save it. Pasta should be cooked to the "al dente" stage, which means "firm to the bite." Taste a piece a few minutes before it approaches the recommended cooking time to ensure that it has some chewiness to it. Don't rely just on appearance or the clock. Sample a piece.

And finally, if you can get your hands on some fresh pasta, do so. (Fortunately, it can be found increasingly in towns across the United States.) There is nothing quite like the texture of fresh noodles, and they take only a few minutes to cook. A pound of fresh pasta equals about $3/4$ pound dried (see page 226).

Matching a noodle shape to a sauce can be summed up easily: Thick, chunky-style sauces generally go well with bulky noodles, such as penne, rigatoni, ziti, and lasagne. More delicate, finely textured sauces pair better with strands of pasta, such as spaghetti, linguine, vermicelli, and angel hair. There are sauces whose heaviness lies somewhere in between, and you can have more latitude with these.

See also: Penne with Fried Tofu, Roasted Peppers, and Olives (page 218)

Fresh Fettuccine with Spinach, Red Peppers, and Smoked Cheese

This pasta dish is a knockout, and one of my favorite recipes to serve when company's arriving on short notice. Even a die-hard vegetarian like myself will readily admit that the bacon-like flavor of smoked cheese is hard to resist, and here, it weaves magic. If you can't get fresh pasta, ³/₄ pound dried linguine could be substituted (odd as it may seem, fresh fettuccine and dried linguine are the same width), but a little character will be lost.

Serves 3–4

¹/₄ cup olive oil

4 garlic cloves, minced

1 red bell pepper, cut into thin 2-inch-long strips

1 (1-pound) bunch or 1 (10-ounce) package fresh spinach, stems discarded and leaves washed

¹/₂ teaspoon salt

Generous seasoning freshly ground pepper

1 pound fresh fettuccine

1 cup grated smoked Gouda cheese

1. Bring a large stockpot of water to a boil.

2. Meanwhile heat the olive oil in a large skillet over medium heat. Add the garlic and cook 1 minute. Stir in the pepper and sauté until tender yet crisp, about 7 minutes.

3. Pile on the spinach, and cover the pan. Cook until wilted, about 3 minutes. Stir in the salt and ground pepper. Keep the sauce warm over very low heat.

4. Drop the fresh pasta into the boiling water and cook about 3 minutes, or until al dente. (If you are using dried pasta it will take 7–10 minutes.) Remove ¹/₄ cup of the starchy pasta water and stir it into the sauce. Drain the pasta and toss it with the sauce. Mix in the cheese and serve immediately.

Pasta Equivalents

A pound of uncooked fresh pasta and a pound of uncooked dried pasta are not equivalent because, when cooked, their yield will be different. Uncooked fresh pasta contains moisture and consequently weighs more than dried pasta, cup for cup. Because fresh pasta weighs more, you get less volume per pound. The best way to determine equivalents is by measuring volume. Use the guide below to help you substitute accurately.

Dried linguine	Fresh fettuccine	Yield (volume)
½ pound	10.5 ounces	3 ½ cups cooked
¾ pound	1 pound	5 cups cooked
1 pound	1 pound 5 ounces	7 cups cooked

Fresh Fettuccine with Uncooked Tomato Sauce and Goat Cheese

In the summer months when fat, juicy tomatoes are abundant, nothing beats this pasta dish for flavor and quickness.

Serves 4

6 ripe plum tomatoes, cored and cut into small dice

3 garlic cloves, minced

1 cup chopped fresh basil

½ teaspoon salt

Generous seasoning freshly ground black pepper

⅓ cup olive oil

4 ounces soft mild goat cheese, crumbled

1 pound fresh fettuccine (or ¾ pound dry linguine)

1. Combine the tomatoes, garlic, basil, salt, pepper, olive oil, and goat cheese in a very large bowl and toss gently. Let sit 30–60 minutes.

2. Bring a large stockpot of water to a boil. Drop in the fresh pasta and cook about 3 minutes. Taste to check its texture. It should be al dente, that is, still chewy. (If you are using dried pasta, it will take considerably longer.) Drain thoroughly in a colander.

3. Drop the pasta into the sauce and toss well. Serve immediately.

Linguine with Roasted Red Peppers, Peas, and Pine Nuts

I love the array of colors and textures in this sauce. In a well-stocked kitchen, these ingredients will all be on hand and you can put this sauce together in just a couple of minutes. If Romano cheese is available, you'll find that its assertiveness is delightful with these flavors.

Serves 4

1 pound linguine

$^1/_3$ cup olive oil

4 garlic cloves, minced

$^3/_4$ cup diced roasted red peppers, store-bought or freshly roasted (page 19)

2 tablespoons pine nuts

1$^1/_2$ cups frozen peas, thawed

$^1/_2$ teaspoon salt

Generous seasoning freshly ground pepper

$^1/_2$ cup chopped fresh parsley

$^1/_3$ cup grated Romano (pecorino) (preferably) or Parmesan cheese

1. Bring a large stockpot of water to a boil. Drop in the linguine and cook until al dente, about 7 minutes.

2. Meanwhile heat the olive oil in a medium-size skillet over medium heat. Add the garlic and cook 1 minute. Stir in the red peppers, pine nuts, peas, salt, and pepper and cook 1 minute, stirring often.

3. Remove $^1/_4$ cup of the starchy pasta water and add it to the sauce along with the parsley.

4. Drain the linguine in a colander and place it in a large bowl or return it to the pot. Pour on the sauce, then sprinkle on the cheese. Toss thoroughly and serve.

Tortellini with Fennel, Tomatoes, and Spinach

The mild licorice flavor in fennel is highlighted by this garlicky mélange of vegetables to create a wonderful sauce with a pleasing palette of colors.

Serves 4

$\frac{1}{4}$ cup olive oil

6 garlic cloves, minced

$\frac{1}{8}$ teaspoon crushed red pepper flakes

1 fennel bulb, halved vertically and thinly sliced (reserve feathery sprigs)

2 plum tomatoes, seeded and cubed

5 cups (5 ounces) fresh spinach, stems discarded

$\frac{1}{4}$ teaspoon salt

Generous seasoning freshly ground black pepper

1 pound frozen cheese tortellini

$\frac{1}{4}$ cup grated Parmesan cheese

1 tablespoon finely chopped fennel sprigs (see above)

1. Bring a large stockpot of water to a boil.

2. Heat the oil in a large skillet over medium heat. Add the garlic and red pepper flakes and cook 1 minute. Stir in the fennel and sauté 5 minutes, or until crisp but tender. Add the tomatoes, toss well, and cook 5 minutes, or until the tomato pieces begin to soften.

3. Stir in the spinach, salt, and pepper and toss just until wilted, about 1 minute. Keep the sauce warm over low heat.

4. Drop the tortellini into the boiling water and cook until al dente, that is, tender yet firm, about 5 minutes. Meanwhile check the consistency of the sauce. Depending on the juiciness of your tomatoes, it might need some liquid. If so, remove 2 tablespoons of the starchy pasta water and add it to the sauce. Drain the tortellini thoroughly, then mix it into the sauce along with the cheese. Serve with the chopped fennel sprigs sprinkled on top.

Tortellini with Kale and Garlicky Bread Crumbs

Toasted, buttery bread crumbs mixed with garlic and herbs become a perfect vehicle for flavor when quickly tossed with pasta. Here, with tender juicy kale as a companion, we have a great match.

Serves 4

The Crumbs
1 tablespoon olive oil
2 garlic cloves, minced
1 cup coarse fresh bread crumbs (from about 2 slices bread; see page 19)
1 tablespoon mixed chopped fresh herbs (such as rosemary, thyme, basil, tarragon, parsley)

1 pound kale
3 tablespoons olive oil
4 garlic cloves, minced
$\frac{1}{4}$ teaspoon crushed red pepper flakes
1 pound frozen cheese tortellini
2 teaspoons balsamic vinegar
$\frac{1}{4}$ teaspoon salt
Freshly ground black pepper
2 tablespoons grated Parmesan cheese

1. To prepare the crumbs, heat the oil in a large skillet over medium heat. Add the garlic and cook 30 seconds. Stir in the bread crumbs and toss continuously until the crumbs become golden, about 5 minutes. Stir in the herbs, toss a few times, then scrape the crumbs into a medium-size bowl. Let them cool. Hold on to the skillet for the next step. (The crumbs can be prepared up to 24 hours in advance.)

2. Bring a large stockpot of water to a boil. Prepare the kale by ripping the leafy part off the stems. Gather the leaves into tight bunches and cut them into shreds (chiffonade). Wash them by dunking them in a large bowl of cold water. Remove and drain in a colander.

3. In the skillet in which the crumbs cooked, heat 2 tablespoons of the olive oil over medium heat. Add the garlic and red pepper flakes and cook 30 seconds. In batches add the kale with the water that clings to it and toss to mix with the garlic. Cover the pan tightly and cook, stirring occasionally, until the kale wilts and becomes tender, about 5–7 minutes. Taste the kale for tenderness. There should be a few tablespoons of liquid in the bottom of the pan when done. If it is dry, add a few tablespoons of boiling pasta water.

4. Meanwhile drop the tortellini into the boiling water and cook until tender, about 5 minutes. Drain in a colander.

5. Sprinkle the balsamic vinegar, salt, and pepper on the kale. Mix the tortellini into the kale along with the Parmesan cheese and remaining tablespoon of olive oil. Serve with a generous handful of crumbs on each serving.

Tortellini with Leeks and Cream

This sauce is very simple and elegant. You don't need much cheese or any other additions because the wonderful flavor of leeks carries the dish.

Serves 3–4

2 large leeks
1 tablespoon unsalted butter
½ cup heavy cream
¼ teaspoon salt
Freshly ground black pepper to taste
1 pound frozen cheese tortellini
1 tablespoon grated Parmesan cheese

1. Bring a large stockpot of water to a boil.

2. Meanwhile slice the roots off the leeks, plus all but 2 inches of the green tops. Slice the leeks in half lengthwise. Under cold running water rinse the leeks, thumbing through all the leaves to dislodge any hidden dirt. Do this thoroughly to rid them of *all* their dirt. Thinly slice the leeks. You can use the light green tops, but discard any dark green pieces. You should get about 2½ cups sliced leeks.

3. Melt the butter over medium heat in a large skillet. Add the leeks and sauté until tender, about 10 minutes. Stir frequently, and keep an eye on the leeks so they don't get at all brown.

4. Pour in the cream, salt, and pepper. Heat just until it boils, then turn the heat very low to keep the sauce warm.

5. Drop the tortellini in the boiling water and cook until al dente, about 5 minutes. Drain in a colander, then mix into the sauce along with the Parmesan cheese. Toss and serve.

Rigatoni with Potatoes, Arugula, and Tomatoes

Pairing pasta with potatoes, as the Genoese do in their regional dish Trenette with Pesto and Potatoes, makes a hearty dish. The potatoes soak up the garlicky sauce and thereby provide little bursts of flavor. This rustic treatment of pasta is utterly satisfying.

Serves 4

$\frac{1}{4}$ cup olive oil

1 large boiling (waxy) potato, peeled and cut into $\frac{1}{2}$-inch dice

1 pound rigatoni

6 garlic cloves, minced

1 (16-ounce) can tomatoes with their juice, finely diced

$\frac{1}{2}$ teaspoon salt

Generous seasoning freshly ground black pepper

1 bunch arugula, coarse stems discarded and leaves cut in half (3–4 cups lightly packed)

$\frac{1}{4}$ cup grated Romano (pecorino) cheese

1. Bring a large stockpot of water to a boil.

2. Meanwhile heat the oil in a medium-size, preferably non-stick, skillet over medium heat. Add the potato and cook until tender and golden, about 10 minutes.

3. When the water boils, drop in the rigatoni. Cook until al dente, about 10 minutes.

4. Meanwhile add the garlic to the potatoes and cook 1 minute. Do not let it color. Stir in the tomatoes, salt, and pepper and cook 2 minutes. Mix in the arugula and cook 1 minute, or until wilted.

5. Drain the rigatoni and place it in a large pasta bowl or return it to the pot. Pour on the sauce, then sprinkle on the cheese. Toss and serve.

Ziti with Cauliflower, Tomatoes, and Hot Peppers

Tomatoes, garlic, and hot peppers bring out the best in cauliflower. This is an electrifying and delicious pasta dish.

Serves 4

3 tablespoons olive oil
6 garlic cloves, minced
¼ teaspoon crushed red pepper flakes
1 (16-ounce) can tomatoes, finely diced with their juice
1 small (about 1½ pounds) cauliflower, cut into tiny florets
½ teaspoon salt
1 pound ziti
2 tablespoons minced fresh parsley
3 tablespoons grated Parmesan cheese

1. Bring a large stockpot of water to a boil.
2. Heat the olive oil in a large skillet over medium heat. Add the garlic and hot pepper flakes and cook 1 minute. Do not let the garlic brown at all. Mix in the tomatoes and their juice, then stir in the cauliflower and salt. Toss well and cover the pan. Cook until the cauliflower is tender, about 5 minutes.
3. Drop the ziti into the boiling water and cook until al dente. Taste one to test it.
4. Drain the ziti in a colander and return it to the pot, or place it in a large pasta bowl. Pour on the sauce, toss, then sprinkle on the parsley and Parmesan cheese. Serve immediately.

Penne with Chunky Sun-Dried Tomato and Black Olive Pesto

Choose your favorite olives to mix into this pesto. In a pinch I have even used canned, "California-style" black olives and had good results. This pesto packs a punch, so all you need for this simply delicious, yet hearty sauce is some pasta to toss it on.

Serves 4

2 ounces (about 13) loose sun-dried tomatoes
⅓ cup olive oil
2 garlic cloves, finely chopped
3 tablespoons pine nuts
⅔ cup chopped fresh parsley
½ teaspoon salt
Freshly ground black pepper to taste
½ cup pitted black olives (page 95)
3 tablespoons grated Parmesan cheese
1 pound penne

1. Steam the tomatoes in a vegetable steamer until they are soft and tender, about 10 minutes. Remove from the pot and let cool.
2. In a food processor combine the tomatoes, oil, and garlic and process until it is the texture of coarse crumbs. Add the pine nuts, parsley, salt, and pepper and process until somewhat smooth but with bits still visible. Add the olives and pulse just a few times to chop them into small pieces. Scrape the pesto into a bowl, then stir in the cheese by hand. (You can prepare the pesto up to 4 days in advance. Cover and chill until ready to use.)
3. Bring a large stockpot of water to a boil. Drop in the penne and cook until al dente. Remove ½ cup of the starchy pasta water and stir it into the pesto.
4. Drain the penne. Toss it with the pesto and serve. I prefer it served warm, not piping hot.)

Penne with Yellow Peppers, Tomatoes, and Black Olives

If it's true that we also eat with our eyes, then both the colors and flavors in this striking treatment will wonderfully satisfy us. The "bite" of Romano cheese juxtaposed with the sweetness of the yellow peppers works well here.

Serves 4

$\frac{1}{3}$ cup olive oil

1 yellow bell pepper, cut into strips 2 × $\frac{1}{2}$ inch

6 garlic cloves, minced

$\frac{1}{4}$ teaspoon crushed red pepper flakes

4 plum tomatoes, cut into 1-inch cubes

15–20 black olives (your favorite kind), pitted and halved (page 95)

1 pound penne

$\frac{1}{2}$ cup chopped fresh basil or parsley

$\frac{1}{4}$ teaspoon salt

$\frac{1}{4}$ cup grated Romano cheese plus extra for serving

1. Bring a large stockpot of water to a boil.

2. Heat the oil in a large skillet over medium heat. Add the yellow pepper and sauté 5 minutes, or until tender yet still crunchy.

3. Add the garlic and hot pepper flakes and cook 2 minutes. Stir in the tomatoes and olives and cook 5 minutes, stirring often. Keep warm over low heat while the pasta cooks.

4. Drop the penne into the boiling water and cook until al dente, about 10 minutes. Remove 2 tablespoons of the starchy pasta water and stir it into the tomatoes along with the basil and salt.

5. Drain the penne thoroughly and return it to the pot, or place it in a large bowl. Stir in the vegetable mixture and Romano cheese. Serve with extra cheese to pass at the table.

Penne with Portobello Mushrooms

Slices of juicy portobello mushrooms make this pasta dish both substantial and elegant. Choose portobellos that are very firm and fresh for best results.

Serves 4 generously

1 pound penne

2 tablespoons olive oil

3/4 pound portobello mushrooms, sliced 1/2 inch thick

4 garlic cloves, minced

3 plum tomatoes, seeded and diced

1 cup frozen peas, thawed

1/2 cup heavy cream

1 tablespoon chopped fresh basil, or 1/2 teaspoon dried

1/4 teaspoon salt

Generous seasoning freshly ground black pepper

1/4 cup grated Parmesan cheese

1. Bring a large stockpot of water to a boil. Drop in the penne and cook until al dente, about 10 minutes.

2. Meanwhile heat the oil in a large skillet over medium heat. Add the mushrooms and sauté until brown, juicy, and cooked throughout, about 10 minutes. Stir often.

3. Add the garlic, toss, and cook 2 minutes. Stir in the tomatoes and peas and cook 2 minutes, or until the tomatoes are hot throughout. Mix in the cream, basil, salt, and pepper and boil 1 minute.

4. Drain the penne and return it to the pot, or place it in a large pasta bowl. Pour on the sauce, sprinkle on the Parmesan cheese, then toss. Serve immediately.

Angel Hair with Spinach and Feta Cheese in Garlic Sauce

Garlic lovers, take note of this captivating sauce, which also features feta cheese in a notable, but not overpowering way.

Serves 4

¼ cup olive oil

8 garlic cloves, minced

½ teaspoon crushed red pepper flakes

3 tablespoons finely chopped walnuts

1 (1-pound) bunch or 1 (10-ounce) package fresh spinach, washed thoroughly, stems discarded, and leaves torn into small pieces, or 1 (10-ounce) package frozen chopped spinach, thawed and squeezed dry

½ teaspoon salt

¾ cup milk

1 pound angel hair pasta

4 ounces crumbled feta cheese (about ¾ cup)

2 tablespoons Romano (pecorino) cheese

1. Bring a large stockpot of water to a boil.

2. Meanwhile heat the oil in a large skillet over medium heat. Add the garlic, red pepper flakes, and walnuts and cook 1 minute, stirring frequently.

3. Pile on the spinach and immediately cover the pan. Cook just until the spinach wilts, about 3 minutes. (If you are using frozen spinach, just stir it into the garlic mixture.) Use tongs to toss the spinach with the garlic mixture. Mix in the salt and milk and keep the sauce warm over low heat.

4. Drop the angel hair into the pot and cook until al dente. Drain thoroughly and return it to the pot or place it in a large pasta bowl. Pour on the sauce, then sprinkle on the feta and Romano cheeses. Toss and serve.

Spaghettini with Garlic, Hot Peppers, and Toasted Bread Crumbs

The garlicky sauce in this humble pasta rendition will have you licking your lips and asking for more. You don't need Parmesan cheese in this case because the bread crumbs do the trick.

Serves 2

4 tablespoons olive oil

1 cup coarse fresh bread crumbs (from about 2 slices bread; see page 19)

½ pound spaghettini

6 garlic cloves, finely chopped

¼ teaspoon crushed red pepper flakes

2 plum tomatoes, cored and diced

1 cup chopped fresh parsley

¼ teaspoon salt

1. Bring a large stockpot of water to a boil.

2. Meanwhile heat 1 tablespoon of the oil in a medium or large skillet over medium heat. Add the bread crumbs and cook, tossing frequently, until they begin to get golden, about 5 minutes. Scrape them into a bowl and set aside.

3. Drop the spaghettini into the boiling water and cook until al dente, about 8–9 minutes. Heat the remaining 3 tablespoons of oil in the same skillet the bread crumbs were cooked in. Add the garlic and crushed red pepper flakes and cook 1 minute. Stir in the tomatoes and sauté 1 minute. Mix in the parsley, salt, and ¼ cup of the starchy pasta water. Remove from the heat.

4. Drain the spaghettini and return it to the pot or place it in a large bowl. Pour on the sauce and toss well. Serve with half the bread crumbs sprinkled on each serving.

Macaroni and Cheese

This is a stove-top version of the favorite American classic. It is just as kids would want it—smooth, creamy, and untouched by any adult embellishments—just macaroni and a silky cheese sauce. Do not turn this into a casserole and bake it, for the cheese will clump and lose its creaminess.

Serves 4

2 large eggs

$^1/_2$ teaspoon Dijon-style mustard

A few dashes cayenne

$^3/_4$ teaspoon salt

1 (12-ounce) can evaporated milk

1 pound elbow macaroni

2 tablespoons unsalted butter, cut into bits

8 ounces (2 $^1/_2$–3 cups) grated extra-sharp Cheddar cheese

$^1/_4$ cup grated Parmesan cheese

1. Bring a large stockpot of water to a boil.

2. Meanwhile beat the eggs, mustard, cayenne, and salt together in a large measuring cup or bowl. Beat in the evaporated milk.

3. Cook the macaroni until al dente. Taste one to be sure. Drain it in a colander and shake well to remove all the water. Return the macaroni to the pot and place it over low heat. Add the butter and stir until it has melted.

4. Pour on the milk mixture, sprinkle on the cheeses, then stir until the cheeses have melted and the sauce has thickened slightly. Serve immediately. The sauce will get too firm if left too long.

Note: To reheat any leftover macaroni and cheese, heat a bit of milk in a saucepan until very hot. Add the leftover macaroni and stir until piping hot.

Potato Gnocchi and Mushrooms in Gorgonzola Sauce

A little Gorgonzola (or other blue cheese) goes a long way to create a robust sauce for these hearty gnocchi. Look for potato gnocchi in the frozen pasta section of your supermarket; they are usually additive-free, and made with only a few simple ingredients.

Serves 2–3

1 tablespoon olive oil
12 ounces mushrooms, thinly sliced (about 4 1/2 cups)
1 pound frozen potato gnocchi
2 garlic cloves, minced
1/4 cup milk
3 ounces Gorgonzola or other blue cheese, cut into small dice
2 tablespoons minced fresh parsley
1/4 teaspoon salt
Generous seasoning freshly ground black pepper

1. Bring a large stockpot of water to a boil.
2. Meanwhile heat the oil in a large skillet over medium-high heat. Add the mushrooms and sauté until they render their juices, then reabsorb them and begin to get dry, about 10 minutes. Stir often.
3. Drop the gnocchi into the boiling water and cook until tender, about 7 minutes.
4. Add the garlic to the mushrooms and cook 2 minutes, tossing frequently. Pour in the milk and bring to a boil. Stir in the blue cheese, parsley, salt, and pepper and toss.
5. Drain the gnocchi and add it to the skillet. Toss 1 minute, or just until the cheese melts. Serve immediately.

Potato Gnocchi with Swiss Chard and Garlic

Garlic and greens were made for each other, as this aromatic sauce demonstrates. Feel free to substitute spinach, kale, escarole, or broccoli rabe and you'll still have a winner.

Serves 2–3

1 pound Swiss chard (weight with stems)

3 tablespoons olive oil

4 garlic cloves, minced

¼ teaspoon crushed red pepper flakes

¼ teaspoon salt

Freshly ground black pepper

1 pound frozen potato gnocchi (see Potato Gnocchi and Mushrooms in Gorgonzola Sauce, page 241)

2 tablespoons grated Parmesan cheese

1. Bring a large stockpot of water to a boil.

2. Meanwhile chop the stems off the chard. Rinse the stems under cold running water to rid them of any sand. Chop them into ½-inch pieces and set them aside. Wash the greens by dunking them in a large bowl of cold water. Remove the leaves, then dump out the water. Repeat until there is no sandy sediment in the water. Drain the greens. Gather the leaves into bunches and slice them into ½-inch-wide strips.

3. Heat the olive oil in a large skillet over medium heat. Add the garlic and hot pepper flakes and cook 1 minute. Add the chard stems and leaves with just the water that clings to them. Toss with the garlic, then cover the pan. Cook, tossing occasionally, just until the chard is wilted, about 3 minutes. Season with the salt and pepper.

4. Drop the gnocchi into the boiling water. Cook according to the package directions, probably about 5 minutes. Drain thoroughly, then mix into the chard. Sprinkle on the cheese, toss, and serve.

Spicy Thai-Style Noodles

Thai cooking is noted for its contrasting combinations of sweet, hot, sour, salty, and bitter flavors. These forces come together to make a beguiling sauce in this special noodle dish, which is one of my all-time favorites.

Although the list of ingredients is long, these noodles are very easy to prepare and are a great choice for entertaining because of their noteworthy flavor and vivid color.

Serves 4

The Sauce

1/4 cup natural-style peanut butter, chunky or smooth

3 tablespoons tamari soy sauce

3 tablespoons tomato sauce or tomato puree

3 tablespoons dry sherry

Grated zest of 1 lime

2 tablespoons lime juice

2 tablespoons brown sugar

1/2–1 teaspoon chili paste with garlic (see Note)

2 tablespoons canola oil

4 garlic cloves, minced

The Vegetable Mixture

2 tablespoons finely chopped roasted peanuts

2 scallions, very thinly sliced

1 small red bell pepper, very finely diced

10 snow peas, cut diagonally into thin shreds

1 pound spaghetti

1. Bring a large stockpot of water to a boil.

2. Place the peanut butter in a medium-size bowl. With a whisk or fork stir in the soy sauce, tomato sauce, sherry, lime zest, lime juice, brown sugar, and chili paste.

3. Heat the oil in a small saucepan over medium heat. Add the garlic and cook 1 minute. Stir in the peanut sauce and keep warm over low heat. Do not let the sauce in any way simmer or boil or it will get too thick; it just needs to be slightly warmed. (The sauce may be prepared to this point up to 6 hours in advance. Reheat when ready to combine with the pasta.)

4. Combine the peanuts, scallions, red pepper, and snow peas in a small bowl and set aside.

5. Drop the spaghetti into the boiling water and cook until the noodles are tender yet still chewy and slightly firm, about 7 minutes. Drain in a colander and return to the pot or place in a large bowl. Pour on the sauce and toss with the noodles. Sprinkle on the vegetable mixture and mix again. Serve immediately.

Note: Chili paste with garlic is a Chinese condiment available in specialty stores, health food stores, and many supermarkets.

Noodles with Cashews
in Curried Coconut Sauce

This wondrous sauce takes only a few minutes to make, yet has great depth and complexity. You can prepare the sauce well in advance and come dinnertime, all you'll need to do is cook the pasta. Do serve these noodles in bowls, Asian-style; it adds to their charm.

Serves 4

1 tablespoon canola oil

3 garlic cloves, minced

2 teaspoons minced gingerroot

2 teaspoons ground coriander

1 1/2 teaspoons ground cumin

1/2 teaspoon turmeric

1/4 teaspoon ground cardamom

1/8 teaspoon cayenne pepper

1 (14-ounce) can unsweetened coconut milk (see Note)

2 tablespoons lemon juice

1 teaspoon salt

1 pound spaghettini

4 scallions, very thinly sliced

1/2 cup coarsely chopped dry-roasted cashews

1 1/2 tablespoons minced cilantro (optional)

1. Bring a large stockpot of water to a boil.

2. To make the sauce, heat the oil in a small saucepan over medium heat. Add the garlic and gingerroot and cook 1 minute. Do not let the garlic get brown. Stir in the coriander, cumin, turmeric, and cayenne and cook 1 minute.

3. Slowly whisk in the coconut milk until it is smooth and well blended. Stir in the lemon juice and salt and heat until hot.

4. Cook the spaghettini until al dente, that is, still somewhat chewy. Drain thoroughly

and return it to the pot. Pour on the sauce, then sprinkle on the scallions and cashews. With tongs toss to evenly coat the noodles. Serve in bowls with some cilantro sprinkled on top, if desired.

Note: Coconut milks vary in thickness. The final sauce should be the consistency of heavy cream, no thicker. If the sauce is too thick, add a few tablespoons of water.

Spicy Peanut Noodles

My friend Darra Goldstein, in her wonderful cookbook *The Vegetarian Hearth,* has a fabulous recipe for Spicy Soba that haunted me for days after I prepared it. Here is my rendition with a few changes from the original. You are likely to have all these ingredients on hand and will be able to put this together in minutes. If you happen to have soba (buckwheat noodles) in your larder, however, try it with them for a tantalizing marriage of flavors.

This has become a staple dish in our house because it's so quick to prepare and utterly satisfying.

Serves 3–4

1/4 cup natural-style peanut butter

1/3 cup tamari soy sauce

2 tablespoons water

1/3 cup firmly packed light brown sugar

1/4 cup oriental sesame oil

2 garlic cloves, put through a press or minced

1 teaspoon minced gingerroot

1/2 teaspoon crushed red pepper flakes

6 scallions, thinly sliced (set aside 2 tablespoons for garnish)

1 pound thin spaghetti

1. Bring a large stockpot of water to a boil.

2. Meanwhile whisk together the peanut butter and tamari in a small saucepan. Stir in all of the remaining ingredients—except the reserved scallions and the spaghetti—until smooth. Put a low heat under the pot to warm the sauce.

3. Drop the spaghetti into the boiling water and cook until al dente. Don't overcook the pasta; it should remain chewy. Drain thoroughly in a colander and return it to the pot. Pour on the sauce and toss. Serve in bowls and garnish with the remaining scallions.

Do-Ahead Casseroles, Gratins, and Tians

Often a one-dish meal that has been made well in advance and needs only to be popped in the oven come mealtime is the perfect solution for your busy schedule. So if the end of the day is when the crunch is on, and you have some time to cook earlier in the day, you'll benefit from selecting a do-ahead recipe out of this chapter.

Some of these casseroles are composed of raw vegetables with little or no precooking involved (tians), and some require more attention, like cooking pasta or making a sauce, but whatever the case, these are ideal cool-weather dishes that will fill your house with warmth and aroma.

White Bean and Vegetable Gratin

This aromatic gratin has become my favorite bean dish. Under a blanket of buttery crumbs is a brightly colored concoction of beans, vegetables, and herbs that creates delectable juices to be sopped up with some crusty French bread. To get these juices you must use ripe tomatoes and very tender white beans; home-cooked beans that are too firm will absorb all the rendered juices and make the mixture dry. Keep an eye on the gratin during the last 15 minutes of cooking. If it appears dry, add a little vegetable stock or thin tomato liquid (the liquid present in canned tomatoes is good) and let it bake with the bean mixture for the remaining 15 minutes. This will thicken the liquid and allow it to blend with the other flavors.

Serves 3–4

2 cups (6 ounces) green beans, each cut in half

4 cups freshly cooked or canned small white beans, such as navy or Great Northern (rinsed thoroughly and well drained if canned)

3 ripe tomatoes, seeded and quartered

1 small red onion, quartered vertically, sections separated

1 yellow bell pepper, cored and cut into 1½-inch chunks

2 small jalapeño peppers (see Note), seeded and minced, or ¼ teaspoon crushed red pepper flakes

5 garlic cloves, roughly chopped

¼ cup olive oil

1 teaspoon chopped fresh thyme, or ½ teaspoon dried

Salt

Generous seasoning freshly ground black pepper

The Topping

1 cup fresh bread crumbs (from about 2 slices bread; see page 19)

1 tablespoon olive oil

1. Preheat the oven to 375 degrees.

2. Steam the green beans until crunchy and bright green, though not yet tender, about 5 minutes.

3. In a large bowl combine the green beans with all the remaining ingredients *except* those for the topping. Toss well, then place in a 2½-quart gratin dish or other shallow casserole. Pat down the top to make it smooth.

4. In a small bowl combine the bread crumbs with the 1 tablespoon oil and mix to coat evenly. Sprinkle the crumbs all over the casserole, then cover the dish with foil. (The gratin may be prepared to this point up to 8 hours in advance.)

5. Bake, covered, for 30 minutes. Remove the foil and bake 30 more minutes. Let sit 10 minutes before serving.

Note: Wear rubber gloves when handling chili peppers.

Gratins

In the United States "au gratin" has become synonymous with cheese sauce, but this is a misuse of the words. In French cooking, gratin simply means "crusted." (In colloquial French *le gratin* refers to the "upper crust" of society.)

A gratin is several ingredients that are placed in a shallow baking dish so that there is a lot of surface exposed. The ingredients are then sprinkled with bread crumbs, or cheese, or are mixed into a white sauce and baked until the characteristic "crust" is formed. Even a fruit dessert can be cooked "au gratin," with sugar and butter or cream melding to form a crunchy topping. Few people can resist a sizzling, golden-topped dish fresh out of the oven, and that accounts for the great appeal of something "gratinéed."

A gratin is also the name of the oval, earthenware baking dish that these crusty creations have been cooked in, so that a "gratin" refers to the preparation inside the dish as well as the baking dish itself.

Penne and Cauliflower Gratin in Tomato-Cream Sauce

Here's an upscale yet homey version of macaroni and cheese with a lighter touch and deeper flavor. The sauce is unusually quick to prepare and the final result very tasty.

Serves 4

1 small cauliflower, cut into small florets (about 4 cups florets)
½ pound penne
1¼ cups chunky tomato sauce, store-bought or homemade
1 cup light cream (or ½ cup heavy cream and ½ cup low-fat milk)
1 garlic clove, put through a press or minced
¼ teaspoon crushed red pepper flakes
½ cup finely chopped fresh basil or parsley
¼ cup grated Parmesan cheese
¼ teaspoon salt
½ cup fresh bread crumbs (made from 1 slice bread)
1 tablespoon olive oil

1. Bring a large pot of water to a boil. Drop in the cauliflower and cook 5 minutes, or just until tender. Scoop it out with a strainer and drop it into a 2½-quart casserole.

2. Drop the penne into the water and cook until al dente, about 10 minutes. Drain it in a colander and shake to remove all the moisture. Mix it into the cauliflower.

3. Preheat the oven to 400 degrees. In a large bowl mix together the tomato sauce, cream, garlic, red pepper flakes, basil or parsley, cheese, and salt. Pour the sauce on the pasta and toss well. (If you don't plan to bake the gratin right away, pour on just one third of the sauce and toss. You can prepare it to this point up to 4 hours in advance. Just before baking pour on the remaining sauce and toss again.)

4. Combine the bread crumbs and olive oil in a small bowl and mix until evenly moistened. Sprinkle all over the gratin. Bake 20–25 minutes, or until hot, bubbly, and golden on top. Let sit 5 minutes before serving.

Potato, Spinach, and Feta Cheese Gratin

Here's a good choice for a blustery evening when you want a hearty casserole that will warm your bones.

Serves 4

1 (1-pound) bunch or 1 (10-ounce) bag fresh spinach, well washed and stems removed, or
    1 (10-ounce) package frozen chopped spinach, thawed
Unsalted butter for greasing dish plus 2 tablespoons
5 medium-large (2½ pounds) boiling (waxy) potatoes, peeled and *very* thinly sliced
Salt
Freshly ground black pepper to taste
4 ounces (about ¾ cup) crumbled feta cheese
2 scallions, very thinly sliced
1 tablespoon minced fresh dill, or 1 teaspoon dried
1¼ cups low-fat milk

1. Place the washed, fresh spinach in a large pot. Cover the pot and cook the spinach over medium heat just until it begins to wilt and is still slightly firm, about 1 minute. (You want to cook it as little as possible because it will bake later.) Put the spinach in a strainer and press out as much liquid as possible with the back of a large spoon. Set the spinach aside. If you are using frozen spinach, just place it in the strainer and extract the liquid.

2. Preheat the oven to 425 degrees. Butter a 2½-quart shallow baking dish.

3. Spread half the potatoes in the baking dish. Season with salt and pepper, then top with the spinach, feta cheese, scallions, and dill. Layer on the remaining potato slices, pour the milk all over the potatoes, then dot the gratin with the remaining 2 tablespoons of butter cut into bits.

4. Cover the dish with foil. Bake 30 minutes. Remove the foil and bake 30 more minutes, or until the potatoes are tender and golden brown on top.

Rice and Leek Gratin

If you have leftover rice, this dish is especially easy to prepare. If you must cook the rice for it, do all the preparatory work in the recipe while the rice is cooking and you'll be able to assemble the casserole by the time the rice is cooled.

Serves 4

The Rice
2$\frac{1}{4}$ cups vegetable stock, store-bought or homemade (page 13)
1 cup basmati or converted white rice
Dash salt
1 teaspoon canola oil

3 large leeks
Unsalted butter for greasing dish, plus 1 tablespoon
1 teaspoon sugar
1 tomato, seeded and very finely diced
$\frac{1}{2}$ teaspoon chopped fresh thyme, or $\frac{1}{4}$ teaspoon dried
$\frac{1}{2}$ teaspoon salt
Freshly ground black pepper to taste
1 egg, beaten
1 cup whole milk
1 cup (3 ounces) grated Gruyère or other Swiss cheese
1 slice bread
1 tablespoon olive oil

1. To cook the rice, bring the vegetable stock to a boil in a medium-size saucepan. Add the rice, salt, and oil and lower the heat to a simmer. Cook, uncovered, until all the liquid is absorbed, about 20 minutes. Place the rice in a large bowl and let cool to room temperature.

2. Meanwhile chop almost all of the green tops off the leeks, except for about 2 inches.

Discard the tops. Cut the roots off the leeks, then slice the leeks in half vertically. Under cold running water wash all the sand from the leeks, flipping through each leaf with your fingers to find any hidden dirt. Be thorough; leeks harbor a lot of dirt. Thinly slice the leeks.

3. In a large skillet heat the butter over medium heat. Add the leeks and sauté until tender, about 10 minutes. Stir in the sugar, tomato, and thyme and cook 2 minutes. Let cool to room temperature.

4. Combine the leek mixture with the rice. Mix in the salt, pepper, egg, and milk.

5. Butter a 2- to 2½-quart shallow gratin dish. Spread half of the rice mixture in the bottom of the dish. Top with the cheese. Spread on the remaining rice mixture and smooth over the top.

6. Put the bread in the blender or food processor to make crumbs. Pour them into a small bowl, then stir in the tablespoon of oil to coat them. Sprinkle them all over the casserole. (The gratin may be prepared to this point up to 8 hours in advance. Cover and chill until ready to bake. Bring to room temperature before cooking.)

7. Preheat the oven to 375 degrees. Bake the gratin 35 minutes, or until sizzling and brown on top. Let sit 5 minutes before serving.

Sweet Potato and Vegetable Tian

One of the wonderful by-products of a slow-cooking tian is that your house will be permeated with intoxicating aromas that can help set the stage for a sumptuous peasant-style meal. Crusty Tuscan-style bread will continue the theme.

Rosemary is the herb of choice in this tian because of its compatibility with sweet potatoes. Do go out of your way to include it because it works so well here.

A tian is a Provençal earthenware baking dish and also the name of the finished product of slowly baked vegetables. You can have successful results with any shallow casserole, but the heavier the better.

Serves 4

1 red onion, cut vertically into sixths, sections separated
1 green bell pepper, cut into 1 1/2-inch chunks
12 ounces mushrooms, large ones quartered, medium ones halved
2 plum tomatoes, cored and cut into sixths
3 medium-large sweet potatoes or yams, peeled, quartered lengthwise, and sliced 1/4 inch thick
4 garlic cloves, thinly sliced
2 teaspoons chopped fresh rosemary, or 3/4 teaspoon crumbled dried
1/2 teaspoon salt
Generous seasoning freshly ground black pepper
1/3 cup olive oil

The Topping
3 slices homemade-type white bread
1 tablespoon olive oil

1. Preheat the oven to 375 degrees. Combine all the vegetables, garlic, and rosemary in a large mixing bowl. Sprinkle on the salt, pepper, and 1/3 cup olive oil and toss to coat thoroughly. (The vegetables may be prepared to this point up to 4 hours in advance.)

2. Drop the vegetables into a shallow 2½-quart ovenproof casserole and press them down evenly. Bake 45 minutes.

3. To make the topping, break up the bread and make coarse crumbs in a food processor. Scrape them into a small bowl and drizzle on the 1 tablespoon of olive oil. Use your fingers to rub the oil evenly into the crumbs.

4. Remove the tian from the oven. Sprinkle the crumbs all over the top. Return the dish to the oven and bake 15 more minutes, or until the vegetables are very tender. Let sit 10 minutes before serving.

Tians

A tian (pronounced TEE-ahn) is a Provençal specialty of vegetables and seasonings cloaked in olive oil and cooked slowly in a hot oven until succulent and tender. "Tian" refers to the method of cooking as well as the heavy baking dish that contains the mélange of ingredients.

In the past, French village bakers would allow home cooks to place their heavy, vegetable-filled tians into still-hot ovens once the last breads were removed. The remaining heat became trapped in the earthenware casseroles and gently cooked the vegetables until they were suffused with the surrounding flavors of a fruity olive oil and aromatic herbs.

When warm weather sets in, it is not uncommon for the French to serve this versatile dish cold, and to tote it along on a picnic. And although it is customary to prepare a simplified tian as a side dish, I love to expand them into one-dish meals. Served with a crusty baguette and some great wine, it's a feast both rustic and sublime.

Cauliflower and Potato Tian

When winter is howling at your door and you want to fill your house with the warmth and bewitching aromas of a slow-cooked, garlicky casserole, choose this homey dish. In India, cauliflower and potatoes are often paired in side dishes and main courses because they enhance each other. Here, a tomato, olive oil, and basil coating gives them a pink hue and a seductive flavor.

Serves 3–4

1 medium (2 pounds) cauliflower, separated into small florets (6 cups florets)

3 medium red-skinned potatoes, quartered lengthwise and sliced ¼ inch thick

4 garlic cloves, finely chopped

¼ cup finely chopped fresh parsley

1 tablespoon finely chopped fresh basil, or ½ teaspoon dried

¼ cup tomato paste

¼ cup olive oil

¼ cup dry white wine or vegetable stock, store-bought or homemade (page 13)

¼ cup water

¼ teaspoon salt

Generous seasoning freshly ground black pepper

The Topping

2 slices homemade-style white bread

1 tablespoon olive oil

¼ cup grated Parmesan cheese

1. Preheat the oven to 400 degrees.

2. In a large bowl combine the cauliflower, potatoes, garlic, parsley, and basil.

3. In a small bowl beat together the tomato paste, olive oil, wine, water, salt, and pepper. Pour it on the vegetables and toss thoroughly to evenly coat them. Scrape this mixture into a 2½-quart shallow ovenproof casserole. Cover with foil. Bake 45 minutes.

4. Meanwhile make the topping by placing the bread in a food processor or blender and processing to make fresh bread crumbs. Pour them into a bowl, then drizzle on the tablespoon of olive oil. Toss thoroughly to distribute the oil.

5. After the casserole has cooked for 45 minutes, remove it from the oven and discard the foil. Sprinkle on the Parmesan cheese, then distribute the bread crumbs all over the top. Bake 15 more minutes, or until golden brown.

Greens and Bulghur Tian

The contrasting textures of the greens are intriguing and delightful here. Kale has a coarse texture, while escarole and spinach are soft and tender. If you love garlicky greens, this casserole is for you, and the bonus is it's filled with calcium and iron. I was surprised to discover how delicious this tian is cold, so consider taking leftovers to work for lunch, or bringing the tian on a picnic.

A note on organization: If you wash the greens early in the day or at least a few hours before you prepare the entire recipe, you'll find this simplifies the whole process considerably.

Serves 4 as a main course

½ cup bulghur, preferably coarse- cut

2 pounds mixed fresh greens, such as kale, escarole, spinach, and Swiss chard

3 tablespoons olive oil, plus extra for greasing dish

6 garlic cloves, minced

Salt

Freshly ground black pepper to taste

¼ cup grated Parmesan cheese

1 cup grated part-skim mozzarella cheese

The Topping

½ cup fresh bread crumbs (from about 1 slice bread; see page 19)

1 tablespoon olive oil

1. Place the bulghur in a medium-size bowl and pour in enough boiling water to cover the bulghur by 1 inch. Cover the bowl with a plate and let sit 20 minutes. Strain the bulghur, pressing out the excess liquid with the back of a large spoon. Set the bulghur aside.

2. Tear the greens into bite-size pieces and discard the stems. Keep the different greens in separate piles. Thoroughly wash the greens by dunking them in a large pot of cold

water. Remove the greens with your hands, place them in a large bowl or other container, then pour out the sandy water. Repeat until the water no longer has any sandy residue.

3. Place the coarser greens, such as kale, in a large stockpot with only the water that clings to them. Cover and cook just until they begin to wilt. Add the more delicate greens, cover the pot, and cook just until wilted. Drain the greens in a colander, and press out any excess liquid with the back of a large spoon.

4. Heat the olive oil in a large skillet over medium heat. Add the garlic and cook 2 minutes. Do not let it brown. Stir in the greens and bulghur. Season generously with salt and pepper, then stir in the Parmesan cheese. Remove from the heat.

5. Preheat the oven to 400 degrees. Oil a $1\frac{1}{2}$-quart tian, gratin dish, or other similar shallow casserole. Spoon in half of the greens mixture. Sprinkle on the mozzarella cheese. Spread on the remaining greens mixture and smooth over the surface. Combine the topping ingredients and sprinkle over the tian. (The tian may be prepared to this point up to 8 hours in advance. Cover and refrigerate if longer than 1 hour, and bring to room temperature before baking.) Bake, uncovered, for 30 minutes, or until sizzling and brown on top.

Baked Goat Cheese and Tomato Polenta

The essence of tomato is a wonderful counterpoint to the creamy layer of goat cheese in this colorful do-ahead casserole.

Serves 6

The Tomato Filling

1 tablespoon olive oil

4 garlic cloves, minced

1 onion, minced

1 (28-ounce) can whole tomatoes, well drained and finely chopped

Generous seasoning freshly ground black pepper

½ cup chopped fresh basil, or 1 teaspoon dried

The Polenta

Unsalted butter for greasing the dish, plus ½ tablespoon cut into bits

2½ cups vegetable stock, store-bought or homemade (page 13)

1½ cups cornmeal

2 cups cold water

½ teaspoon salt

¼ cup plus 1 tablespoon grated Parmesan cheese

½ cup grated part-skim mozzarella cheese

4 ounces soft mild goat cheese, chilled

1. To make the filling, heat the oil in a medium-size skillet over medium heat. Add the garlic and onion and sauté until soft and golden, about 10 minutes. Stir in the tomatoes, season with the pepper, and cook until the juices thicken and are almost evaporated, about 10 minutes. Stir in the basil, and remove the pan from the heat.

2. To make the polenta, preheat the oven to 400 degrees. Butter a 2- to 2½-quart shallow baking dish and set aside.

3. Bring the vegetable stock to a boil in a 3½-quart saucepan over high heat. Place the

cornmeal in a large bowl and whisk in the cold water. (This method ensures lump-free polenta.) Continue to whisk this mixture while pouring it into the boiling stock. Bring the entire contents to a boil, whisking almost constantly. Once the polenta begins to boil, reduce the heat to medium. Whisk the polenta continuously until it begins to tear away from the sides of the pan, about 5 minutes. Whisk in the salt, $1/4$ cup of the grated Parmesan cheese, and the mozzarella cheese.

4. Immediately pour half the polenta into the prepared baking dish. Quickly spread on the tomato mixture. Crumble the goat cheese evenly over the tomatoes. Immediately spoon on the remaining polenta, covering the entire surface. Sprinkle the top with the remaining tablespoon of Parmesan cheese. Dot with the butter bits.

5. Let the polenta rest at least 15 minutes, or up to 24 hours. If longer than 1 hour, cover and refrigerate. Bring to room temperature before baking. Bake 25 minutes, or until hot and bubbly, and golden on top. Let the polenta sit 15 minutes before serving.

Baked Cheese Polenta
with Swiss Chard

Although I'm partial to chard in this melt-in-your-mouth casserole, other greens would work, such as spinach, kale, escarole, or broccoli rabe. Have everything laid out in front of you before you begin cooking to allow you to smoothly run through these steps.

Serves 4

1 tablespoon olive oil

6 garlic cloves, minced

8–10 cups chopped Swiss chard, stems and leaves kept separate

The Polenta

Butter for greasing dish, plus 1 tablespoon butter

2 cups low-fat milk

1 1/2 cups water

1/2 teaspoon salt

1 cup cornmeal

3 tablespoons grated Parmesan cheese

1 cup grated part-skim mozzarella cheese

1/3 cup sour cream

1. Heat the oil in a large skillet over medium heat. Add the garlic and cook 30 seconds, then stir in the Swiss chard stems. Pour in a few tablespoons of water and cover the pan. Cook the stems 2 minutes. Remove the cover, then mix in the Swiss chard leaves. Cover the pan again and cook until the leaves wilt, about 3 minutes. Toss occasionally. Remove the pan from the heat and let cool, uncovered.

2. To make the polenta, preheat the oven to 400 degrees.

3. Butter a 2- to 2 1/2-quart shallow baking dish and set it nearby. Combine the milk, water, and salt in a medium-size saucepan and bring to a boil. Reduce the heat to medium-low and slowly drizzle in the cornmeal, whisking all the while with a wire whisk. Continue to cook and whisk the polenta until it is the consistency of mashed

potatoes and tears away from the sides of the pan, about 5 minutes. Whisk in 2 tablespoons of the Parmesan cheese, the 1 tablespoon butter, and the mozzarella cheese.

4. Spread half of the polenta in the baking dish. Spoon on the Swiss chard and distribute it evenly. Drop on small spoonfuls of the sour cream and spread it with the back of a spoon. Spoon on the remaining polenta and spread it out. Sprinkle on the remaining tablespoon of Parmesan cheese. (The casserole may be prepared to this point and refrigerated up to 24 hours in advance. Bring to room temperature before baking.)

5. Bake the polenta for 20–25 minutes, or until golden on top and sizzling. Do not overcook it because you want to retain its creamy interior.

Foolproof Polenta

Despite its reputation, polenta can be one of the quickest and easiest dishes to whip up. You don't always need to use stone-ground or coarse cornmeal; a finer grind of cornmeal makes a delicious polenta with a more satiny texture. (Although it is slightly less nutritious because it is degerminated.)

There are two foolproof methods that I use to make polenta. The quickest approach is to bring water or stock to a boil, then *very slowly* drizzle or sprinkle in some fine cornmeal (Quaker Oats is okay), whisking all the while with a wire whisk. Reduce the heat to a simmer, and keep whisking until the polenta has the consistency of soft mashed potatoes and pulls away from the sides of the pot. This will take 5–10 minutes. This is the point to add butter and cheese.

Another method, which takes a bit longer and also guarantees smooth polenta, is to place the cornmeal in your saucepan, then whisk in the required amount of cold water. Turn the heat on under the pot, and whisk the mixture almost constantly until it comes to a boil. Lower the heat, and keep whisking until it is as described above, like soft mashed potatoes.

Baked Pasta Shells with Eggplant

A non-stick skillet allows you to fry eggplant with just a little oil rather than the generous amounts normally used to brown it. While the eggplant is frying and the pasta water is coming to a boil, use this time to prepare the remaining ingredients and you'll have it all ready to assemble by the time the shells are cooked.

Serves 4

4 tablespoons olive oil

1 medium (1¼ pounds) eggplant, peeled and diced (¾-inch dice)

½ pound small pasta shells

6 garlic cloves, minced

¼ teaspoon crushed red pepper flakes

1½ cups canned crushed tomatoes (or tomato puree)

2 tablespoons dry red wine

½ teaspoon salt

½ cup chopped fresh parsley

¼ cup chopped fresh basil, or 1 teaspoon dried

½ cup diced roasted red peppers, store-bought or freshly roasted (page 19)

4 tablespoons grated Parmesan cheese

1½ cups grated part-skim mozzarella cheese

1. Bring a large stockpot of water to a boil. Heat 1 tablespoon of the oil in a large non-stick skillet over medium-high heat. Fry *half* the eggplant, tossing often, until it begins to brown and appears somewhat translucent or shiny. Initially the eggplant will absorb the oil and look dry; don't add any more oil, just keep frying and tossing until its juices are released. When done, the eggplant should be still somewhat firm because it will bake further in the oven. Don't overcook it.

2. Remove the eggplant and place it in a shallow 2½-quart baking dish. Using 1 tablespoon of the oil, fry the second batch of eggplant in the same way.

3. When the pasta water is ready, drop in the shells. Cook until al dente, not mushy.

Drain in a colander, then return to the pot.

4. Place the remaining 2 tablespoons of the oil in the skillet. Add the garlic and hot pepper flakes and cook 1–2 minutes, just until fragrant but not colored. Stir in the tomatoes, wine, salt, parsley, basil, and red peppers. Cook 2 minutes, and remove from the heat.

5. Preheat the oven to 375 degrees.

6. Stir the eggplant, sauce, and 2 tablespoons of the Parmesan cheese into the pasta shells. Place *half* of this mixture in the casserole dish that held the eggplant (you don't need to dirty another dish this way). Top with the mozzarella cheese. Spread the remaining pasta mixture on top, then sprinkle on the remaining 2 tablespoons of Parmesan cheese. Cover the dish with foil. (The casserole can be prepared to this point, covered, and refrigerated up to 24 hours in advance.)

7. Bake 30 minutes, or until hot and bubbly. Remove the foil and bake 5 more minutes.

Spinach, Roasted Red Pepper, and Corn Enchiladas

The wonderfully appealing flavor of cumin enhances the filling in these delicious enchiladas. There is little cooking involved in the assembling of the dish, so you'll be able to put these together quite effortlessly.

Serves 4

The Filling
1 cup low-fat cottage cheese

1 (10-ounce) box frozen chopped spinach, thawed

1 tablespoon olive oil

1 medium onion, minced

½ teaspoon ground cumin

1½ cups frozen corn, thawed

1 (7-ounce) jar roasted red peppers, patted dry and diced (1 cup diced)

2 tablespoons grated Parmesan cheese

¼ teaspoon salt

Freshly ground pepper to taste

½ teaspoon dried oregano

Butter for greasing dish

8 (8-inch) flour (wheat) tortillas

The Sauce
1¼ cups mild or medium salsa

½ cup heavy cream

¼ cup milk

1¼ cups grated Monterey Jack cheese

1. Puree the cottage cheese in a food processor or blender until perfectly smooth. Scrape it into a medium-size bowl.

2. Place the spinach in a strainer and press out all its liquid with the back of a large spoon. Set the spinach aside.

3. Heat the olive oil in a large skillet over medium heat. Add the onion and sauté, stirring frequently, until golden brown and soft, about 10 minutes. Add the cumin and cook 2 minutes to "toast it." Stir in the spinach and cook 2 minutes, tossing frequently. Let the mixture cool, then stir it into the cottage cheese along with all the remaining filling ingredients. (The filling may be prepared and chilled up to 24 hours in advance.)

4. Preheat the oven to 375 degrees. Butter a 9 × 13-inch baking dish, or 2 smaller similar baking dishes. If your tortillas seem dry and might tear easily, use a pastry brush and lightly brush each one on both sides with some water. Divide the spinach mixture into 8 portions and place a portion along the bottom of each tortilla and roll tightly. Place the enchiladas on the counter as you complete them.

5. To make the sauce, combine the salsa, cream, and milk in a small bowl. Spoon a thin layer of the sauce on the bottom of the baking dish. Place the enchiladas in the dish, then spoon on the remaining sauce. Sprinkle some cheese along each enchilada. (The enchiladas may be prepared to this point up to 8 hours in advance. Cover and chill if longer than 1 hour. Bring to room temperature before baking.) Bake, covered, 25 minutes. Remove the cover and bake 5 more minutes, or until golden and bubbly. Let sit 5 minutes before serving.

Desserts

Serving a homemade dessert is a special treat, not a daily occurrence, and so to my mind it better be well worth the time and calories. These sumptuous finales surely are. Here is a selection of desserts to suit every occasion—from elegant entertaining to casual after-school snacks. When choosing a dessert for a menu, keep in mind the structure of the meal. Richness is almost always a primary consideration. If the entree has cheese or cream in it, then select a dessert that is fruit-based or on the light side. If you're serving an Asian-style main course that is dairy-free and low-fat, then this is the time to present a buttery cake or rich, flaky tart. As with so much in life, it's a question of balance.

Caramelized Pear and Ginger Upside-Down Cake

The caramelized layer of pears spiked with candied ginger gives this superb cake its hauntingly good flavor. I prefer Bosc pears because they are so sweet; however, D'Anjou or Comice are acceptable. This is one of my favorite desserts.

Serves 6–8

4 tablespoons unsalted butter
½ cup firmly packed light brown sugar
2 tablespoons finely diced candied (crystallized) ginger
3 small firm but ripe Bosc pears, peeled, cored, and cut into sixths

The Cake
4 tablespoons unsalted butter, softened
1 cup sugar
2 teaspoons vanilla extract
2 eggs
1¼ cups unbleached white flour
1½ teaspoons baking powder
½ teaspoon salt
½ cup milk

Sweetened whipped cream (optional)

1. Preheat the oven to 350 degrees. Melt 4 tablespoons butter in a small saucepan over low heat. Brush some of it on the sides of a 9-inch round cake pan (not a springform). Mix the brown sugar into the butter in the saucepan and stir until melted. Pour the mixture into the cake pan and spread evenly.

2. Place pieces of the candied ginger evenly over the pan. Arrange the pear slices in a circle around the pan in the following way: Lay them on their rounded exteriors with the top tip of each slice pointing toward the center. Chop any remaining pear slices and use the pieces to fill the center of the circle.

3. To make the cake, place the 4 tablespoons of butter plus the sugar and vanilla in a large bowl. With an electric beater cream the mixture until very smooth. Add the eggs and beat until fluffy.

4. Add the flour, baking powder, and salt and beat until combined. Add the milk and beat until smooth. Scrape the batter over the pears and smooth over the top.

5. Place the pan in the oven; place a baking sheet on the rack beneath it to catch any juices that might overflow. Bake 45–55 minutes, or until a knife inserted in the cake comes out clean. The cake will be a deep golden brown when done. Don't worry if the top of the cake isn't picture perfect—it will be turned upside down.

6. Cool on a wire rack for 10 minutes, then loosen the edges by running a knife all around the cake. Lay a platter over the cake and invert. Cool to room temperature before serving as is or with a spoonful of whipped cream beside each piece.

Unsalted Butter

I am frequently asked why I specify unsalted butter in my recipes, then include salt as an ingredient. The reason unsalted butter is preferred is not that I am limiting my salt intake, but that unsalted butter is fresher than the salted variety. Because salt masks rancidity, salted butter has a much longer shelf life than unsalted (sweet) butter, which must always be fresh.

Orange Almond Cake

There are few flavors more beguiling in combination than orange and almond. In addition to this cake's sensational flavor, its texture is so delicate and moist that it practically melts in your mouth. Almond paste greatly contributes to this cake's wonderful character. The final result is a luxurious 1-layer butter cake that needs just a dusting of powdered sugar to finish it off. Simple elegance at its best.

Serves 8

¼ pound (1 stick) unsalted butter, very soft

1 cup sugar

7-8 ounces almond paste (see Note)

2 tablespoons orange liqueur (such as Grand Marnier or triple sec)

Grated zest of 1 orange, or ½ teaspoon orange extract

5 large eggs

½ cup cake flour

1 teaspoon baking powder

Confectioners' sugar for dusting

1. Preheat the oven to 325 degrees. Butter and flour a 9-inch springform pan and set it aside.

2. In a large bowl, using an electric mixer, beat the butter and sugar together until very fluffy, at least 3 minutes. Finely crumble up the almond paste with your fingers, and add it to the bowl along with the orange liqueur and orange zest. Beat until perfectly blended, another 2 minutes or so.

3. One by one beat in the eggs until the mixture is very smooth and fluffy, about 2 minutes. Sprinkle on the flour and baking powder and beat just until combined, 30 seconds or so.

4. Scrape the batter into the prepared pan. Bake 55 minutes, or until a knife inserted in the center of the cake comes out clean and the sides have begun to shrink away from the

pan. Cool on a wire rack for 10 minutes. (The cake might sink a little in the center.)

5. Remove the outer ring of the pan. Place a plate over the cake and invert it. Remove the bottom of the pan. Invert again onto a wire rack. Cool the cake completely. Serve dusted with confectioners' sugar.

Note: Almond paste, usually sold in a log similar to marzipan, can be purchased in most supermarkets and specialty food shops. Almond paste, which has less sugar and more almonds than marzipan, is intended for cooking, while marzipan is intended for icings and confections that don't require baking.

If your almond paste is not easily malleable at room temperature, process it in a food processor until it is the texture of cracked wheat, then add it to your recipe.

Nantucket Cranberry Cake

This delicious cake is a spin-off of a dessert called Nantucket Cranberry Pie. Both desserts are made in a pie plate or quiche dish in which a thin, buttery cake sits atop a layer of sweetened cranberries and walnuts. In my version the topping is lighter in texture and more cake-like, which I feel is an improvement on the original.

You cannot use a springform pan for this dessert because the juices will leak out. Any pie plate or ceramic (or Pyrex) quiche dish that holds 1½ quarts of liquid will do. It should be shallow and about 10 inches in diameter.

This is an ideal dessert for Thanksgiving or Christmas. Dusted with confectioners' sugar and served with espresso, coffee, or tea, you have a sumptuous and easy dessert.

Serves 8

Butter for greasing the dish

The Bottom Layer
2 cups cranberries
½ cup finely chopped (not ground) walnuts
½ cup sugar

The Batter
¼ pound (1 stick) unsalted butter, softened
¾ cup sugar
1 egg
½ teaspoon vanilla extract
¼ teaspoon almond extract
1 cup unbleached flour
1 teaspoon baking powder
¼ teaspoon salt
½ cup milk

Confectioners' sugar for dusting

1. Preheat the oven to 350 degrees. Lightly butter a 1½-quart-capacity pie plate or quiche dish (not with a removable bottom).

2. Arrange the cranberries evenly on the bottom of the dish. Sprinkle on the walnuts and sugar.

3. To make the batter, in a large bowl use an electric mixer to beat the butter and sugar together until light and somewhat fluffy. Add the egg and the vanilla and almond extracts and beat until very smooth and fluffy. Be patient.

4. Sprinkle in the flour, baking powder, and salt and beat a few seconds. Pour in the milk and beat just until incorporated.

5. Using a spoon, drop small mounds of batter all over the cranberries. With a narrow metal icing spatula spread the batter around to evenly cover the berries.

6. Bake 45 minutes, or until the cake springs back when you gently press the center with your finger. (The cake will be a rich golden color.) Cool completely before serving. Place confectioners' sugar in a sieve and dust the top of the cake with it. Cut into wedges and serve.

Chocolate Orange Almond Torte

Favorite ingredients that are highly compatible go beyond the sum of their good flavors to create another dimension in taste. The trinity of chocolate, orange, and almond is one such example of mutually enhancing flavors that excite the palate and linger in one's memory.

This rich, sophisticated, European-style cake, which is about 1-inch high, is a superlative example of that magic in action. Served in small portions with a spoonful of whipped cream on the side, it is a dessert that is utterly gratifying.

Serves 8

6 ounces semi-sweet chocolate, chopped, or 1 cup semi-sweet chocolate chips

3 tablespoons water

$\frac{1}{4}$ pound (1 stick) unsalted butter, cut into small chunks

$\frac{2}{3}$ cup whole almonds

3 eggs

Pinch salt

$\frac{2}{3}$ cup sugar

2 tablespoons Grand Marnier or triple sec

$3\frac{1}{2}$ tablespoons unbleached flour

Grated zest of 1 orange

Confectioners' sugar

Unsweetened or barely sweetened whipped cream (optional)

1. Preheat the oven to 375 degrees. Butter and flour a 9-inch layer pan.

2. Combine the chocolate and water in a medium-size, heavy-bottomed saucepan over medium-low heat and stir almost continuously until melted and blended. Do not let the mixture get too hot or scorch; chocolate does not like high heat. Remove the pan from the heat. Drop in the pieces of butter and stir until blended. Set aside.

3. Finely grind the almonds in a blender or processor. You should get about $\frac{3}{4}$ cup.

4. Separate the eggs, placing the whites in 1 large bowl and the yolks in another large bowl. Beat the egg whites with a pinch of salt until stiff but not dry.

5. Without cleaning the beaters beat the yolks with the sugar until pale and creamy, a good 3 minutes. Beat in the cooled melted chocolate until blended. Beat in the almonds, Grand Marnier, flour, and orange zest just until blended, about 1 minute.

6. With a rubber spatula *stir* one third of the egg whites into the batter to lighten it. Carefully *fold* the remaining egg whites into the batter until they are incorporated. (Do this with a light hand so that the batter isn't overbeaten yet no streaks remain.)

7. Scrape the batter into the prepared pan and bake for 28–30 minutes, or until a knife inserted in the center of the cake comes out almost, but not completely, dry. Do not overbake the cake.

8. Cool on a wire rack for 10 minutes, then invert the cake onto a plate and remove the pan. Let cool completely before serving. Dust lightly with powdered sugar. If desired, serve with a spoonful of whipped cream next to each portion.

Strawberry Almond Cream Cake

This is the perfect summer cake—light and fresh-tasting while amply filled with berries and whipped cream. It's quick to make and its texture is moist and delicate.

I prefer to use a blender rather than a food processor for the batter because it grinds the almonds very fine; however, if a food processor is all you have, you'll still get great results. For the strawberries, you'll need about 1 quart total: 2 cups sliced and the remainder for decorating.

Serves 8

7 eggs

1 teaspoon almond extract

$^1/_2$ teaspoon vanilla extract

1$^1/_2$ cups sugar

1$^1/_4$ cups whole skinless almonds, or 1$^3/_4$ cups slivered almonds, or a scant 2 cups sliced almonds

$^1/_4$ cup plus 2 tablespoons unbleached flour

3$^3/_4$ teaspoons baking powder

The Filling

2 cups thinly sliced fresh strawberries

2 tablespoons strawberry jam

1 teaspoon Grand Marnier, rum, or kirsch

The Topping

1$^1/_2$ cups well-chilled heavy cream

$^1/_4$ cup sugar

1 teaspoon vanilla extract

$^1/_4$ teaspoon almond extract

About 2 cups halved strawberries for decorating

1. Preheat the oven to 350 degrees. Butter 2 (9-inch) cake pans. Line the bottoms with parchment or wax paper and butter the paper. Place your beaters and bowl in the freezer, so they are well chilled for whipping the cream.

2. In a blender combine the eggs, the almond and vanilla extracts, and the sugar and blend until creamy and smooth. Turn off the blender and add the almonds. Blend until very fine, at least 1 minute. Add the flour and baking powder and blend until smooth.

3. Divide the batter between the 2 prepared pans. Bake about 17–18 minutes, or until the cakes are golden brown on top and have begun to shrink from the sides of the pan. The cakes will puff while cooking, and then collapse. When done, they will no longer be "jiggly," but will spring back when touched with your index finger. They'll be only about 1 1/4 inches high.

4. Cool on a wire rack for 5 minutes. Invert the cakes, then remove the pans and parchment paper. Let cool completely.

5. To make the filling, place the 2 cups of sliced strawberries in a large bowl. With a fork mash about one quarter of the berries. Mix in the jam and liqueur. Let sit until you are ready to assemble the cake.

6. When the cake is completely cool, remove the beaters and bowl from the freezer. Place the heavy cream in the cold bowl and whip on high speed until it begins to thicken. Sprinkle in the sugar and vanilla and almond extracts and whip until stiff but not buttery.

7. To assemble the cake, place a layer on a large plate. Spoon the strawberries all over the top, plus about 1/2 cup of the accumulated liquid. (Discard the remaining liquid.) Place the remaining cake layer on top. Cover the entire cake with the whipped cream. Decorate the cake with the strawberry halves. I like to place them on top of the cake along the edge, then create an inner circle in the center, plus a row along the outside bottom edge of the cake.

8. Chill until ready to serve. You can make the entire cake 1 day in advance. Cover it with a cake dome or large inverted pot and refrigerate.

Cassata Siciliana

There are many versions of cassata. What they share is a sweetened ricotta filling and chocolate icing. This easy 3-layer loaf cake resembles a cross between a cannoli and a rum cake. There's virtually no cooking involved and the final product looks stunning. Great for a party.

Do start the cake early in the day so that it has time to chill.

Serves 8

The Syrup

$^1\!/_4$ cup light rum

$^1\!/_4$ cup sugar

3 tablespoons water

The Filling

$1\,^1\!/_2$ cups part-skim ricotta cheese

$^2\!/_3$ cup confectioners' sugar

2 tablespoons semi-sweet chocolate chips, finely chopped

Grated zest of 1 orange

The Ganache (Chocolate Cream Icing)

$^3\!/_4$ cup heavy cream

$^1\!/_2$ cup (about 3 ounces) semi-sweet chocolate chips

1 tablespoon sugar

1 (10-ounce) frozen pound cake, thawed

$^1\!/_3$ cup sliced almonds for decorating

1. To make the syrup, combine the rum, sugar, and water in a small saucepan and bring to a boil, stirring to make sure the sugar has melted. Pour it into a small bowl and let cool.

2. In a medium-size bowl whisk together the ricotta and confectioners' sugar until very smooth. Whisk in the chocolate chips and grated orange zest. Cover and chill until it

becomes a spreadable consistency, not soupy, about 30 minutes.

3. To make the ganache, combine the cream, chocolate, and sugar in a medium-size saucepan. Heat over medium heat, stirring frequently, until the chocolate is blended with the cream. Do not boil the mixture. Pour it into a metal bowl and chill until ice cold, about 2 hours. Stir it occasionally to speed up the process.

4. To assemble the cake, slice the pound cake *lengthwise* into 3 layers. Place the bottom layer on a platter. With a small spoon drizzle one third of the rum syrup all over the layer. Spread on *half* of the ricotta mixture. Top with the second layer of cake and drizzle on one third of the syrup. Spread on the remaining ricotta mixture. Top with the final layer of cake, but flip it over so that the crusted layer is underneath. Spoon on the remaining rum syrup. Cover the cake with plastic wrap and chill a few hours or overnight.

5. To ice the cake, use an electric mixer and whip the icing just until it is spreadable—not soupy or like butter. This will happen rather quickly. Spread the ganache all over the loaf cake. Make an attractive, continuous "S" or "ribbon" pattern on the top of the cake using a knife or thin metal spatula. Press the almonds into the sides of the cake. Chill at least 1 hour or until the icing gets firm. Serve thinly sliced.

Quick Strawberry Shortcake

Here is a fabulous dessert that always gets raves in my house. To make shortcakes quickly, I have developed a method whereby one big almond-flavored "biscuit" is baked and then cut into individual portions, rather than rolling and cutting out separate short-cakes. Although the biscuit is cut into 9 portions, the strawberry and whipped cream amounts are for 4–5 servings. I did this because I imagine most people won't be serving 9 people, and would prefer to freeze the leftover shortcakes for another day. However, if you are serving a large group, just double the strawberry filling and whipped cream top-ping.

Serves 4–5

2 pints strawberries, hulled and thinly sliced

$^1\!/_4$–$^1\!/_3$ cup sugar (depending on the sweetness of the berries)

The Shortcake

$1\,^2\!/_3$ cups unbleached flour

$^1\!/_3$ cup plus 1 tablespoon sugar

1 teaspoon baking powder

$^1\!/_2$ teaspoon baking soda

$^1\!/_4$ teaspoon salt

4 tablespoons chilled unsalted butter, cut into bits

1 large egg

$^2\!/_3$ cup buttermilk or yogurt thinned with a little milk

$^1\!/_2$ teaspoon vanilla extract

$^1\!/_4$ teaspoon almond extract

$^3\!/_4$ cup chilled heavy cream

$1\,^1\!/_2$ tablespoons sugar

$^1\!/_2$ teaspoon vanilla extract

1. Combine the strawberries and sugar in a large bowl, and set aside for at least 1 hour to extract the juices. If longer than an hour, cover and chill.

2. Preheat the oven to 400 degrees. Generously butter an 8 × 8-inch baking pan. To make the shortcake, thoroughly combine the flour, ⅓ cup sugar, baking powder, baking soda, and salt in a large bowl. Drop in the butter, toss to coat it with the flour, then rub it between your fingertips until pea-size crumbs form.

3. Beat the egg in a medium-size bowl. Beat in the buttermilk and the vanilla and almond extracts. Scrape this mixture into the flour mixture, then stir it quickly with a fork just until the flour is evenly moistened. Don't overbeat it. Scrape the dough into the prepared pan and smooth over the top. Sprinkle on the remaining tablespoon of sugar.

4. Bake about 17 minutes, or until a knife inserted in the center of the shortcake comes out clean, and the top is golden. Cool completely on a wire rack.

5. Meanwhile whip the cream with the sugar and vanilla until thick but still somewhat soupy.

6. To serve the strawberry shortcake, cut the biscuit into 9 squares. Freeze 4–5 of them for future use, if desired. Split each biscuit in half horizontally. Spoon some of the strawberries and syrup in the bottom of each serving dish. Place the bottom of the biscuit on the strawberries, then cover with some more strawberries and some whipped cream. Place the top of the biscuit on the berries, and finish with a dollop of whipped cream on top.

Wacky Cake

"Wacky" cake is so called because it has no eggs in it and is mixed together in an unusual way. I have a 2-layer version in *Quick Vegetarian Pleasures* and offer you this adaptation because it is even quicker, and is the ideal chocolate cake to make at a moment's notice when you want something for the family that will go well with a glass of ice-cold milk. It is made in an 8 × 8-inch pan, and covered with a fantastic chocolate glaze. Chocolate cake doesn't get any quicker—or better—than this. Enjoy!

Because it takes only a few minutes to make this cake batter (you don't even have to butter the pan beforehand), you must turn your oven on at least 10 minutes before you begin so it has enough time to preheat.

Serves 6–9

1¼ cups unbleached flour

1 cup sugar

⅓ cup unsweetened cocoa powder

1 teaspoon baking soda

½ teaspoon salt

1 cup warm water

1 teaspoon vanilla extract

⅓ cup vegetable oil

1 teaspoon distilled white or apple cider vinegar

The Chocolate Glaze

½ cup sugar

4 tablespoons unsalted butter

2 tablespoons milk

2 tablespoons unsweetened cocoa powder

2 teaspoons vanilla extract

1. Preheat the oven to 350 degrees.(If you are using a Pyrex baking dish, preheat it to 325 degrees.) A good 10 minutes later, begin to make the cake. Place the flour, sugar,

cocoa, baking soda, and salt in an 8 × 8-inch cake pan. Using a fork, stir the dry ingredients together until *completely* blended and uniform in color with no visible streaks.

2. Pour on the water, vanilla, oil, and vinegar and immediately stir with the fork until completely blended. It's a good idea to use a rubber spatula at this point to help mix the batter that's lodged in the corners.

3. Place the cake in the oven and bake 30 minutes, or until a knife inserted in the center of the cake comes out clean. Cool the cake completely on a wire rack, about 2 hours. (This cake is meant to be served out of the pan, not unmolded.)

4. To make the glaze, combine the sugar, butter, milk, and cocoa in a small saucepan and bring to a boil, stirring frequently. Reduce the heat to a lively simmer and cook 2 minutes, stirring constantly. Remove the pan from the heat and stir until cool, about 5 minutes. Add the vanilla extract, then pour the glaze on the cake. Let cool completely before serving, about 1 hour.

Variations

✣ For a 9 × 13-inch rectangular cake pan, use 1½ times the recipe and cook about 25 minutes.

✣ For a 9-inch round springform pan use 1½ times the recipe and cook about 50 minutes. (Butter and flour the pan beforehand, mix the batter in a large bowl, then pour in the pan. Unmold after baking.)

✣ For a sheet cake use a 17 × 11-inch jelly roll pan that has been buttered and floured beforehand. Mix 3 times the batter in a large bowl, then pour into the prepared pan. Bake about 35 minutes. Unmold after baking.

✣ For cupcakes this recipe will make a dozen. Place 12 paper liners in a muffin pan. Mix the batter in a bowl, then fill the liners. Bake about 22 minutes.

Almond Pound Cake

Pound cake doesn't get any better than this.

Serves 10–12

2 cups unbleached flour

1 teaspoon baking powder

2 sticks (1 cup) unsalted butter, softened

1½ cups sugar

7 ounces almond paste (see Note)

4 large eggs

½ cup milk

Confectioners' sugar for dusting

1. Preheat the oven to 350 degrees. Butter and flour a 10-inch tube pan. Combine the flour and baking powder in a medium-size bowl and set aside.

2. In a large bowl, using an electric mixer, cream together the butter and sugar until very fluffy and smooth.

3. Using your fingers, break up the almond paste into small bits and soften it by rubbing it between your fingers. Drop it into the butter mixture and beat until well incorporated.

4. One by one add the eggs, beating well after each addition.

5. Add a portion of the flour alternately with some of the milk and beat until well incorporated. Repeat until all the flour and milk have been added.

6. Scrape the batter into the prepared pan. Bake about 55 minutes, or until a knife inserted in the center of the cake comes out clean. Cool on a wire rack for 10 minutes, then remove the cake from the pan. Let cool completely, about 2 hours. Sprinkle confectioners' sugar over the top of the cake before serving. To serve, cut into thin slices.

Note: If your almond paste is not malleable at room temperature, process it in a food processor for a minute or so, or until it is the texture of cracked wheat, then add it to your recipe.

Easy Tarte Tatin

This classic French dessert, which is essentially an upside-down caramelized apple tart, is one of the most delicious fruit concoctions ever. By using frozen puff pastry instead of a homemade piecrust, your work is cut down considerably while preserving this dessert's wonderful panache.

Using the right skillet for this dish is essential. I use a 10-inch non-stick ovenproof skillet, which produces perfect results. A cast-iron skillet would work equally well.

Serves 6

1 sheet (½ [17-ounce] box) frozen puff pastry, thawed
Flour for dusting
5 tablespoons unsalted butter
⅔ cup sugar
5 medium-large apples (such as Golden Delicious, Cortland, or Macoun), peeled, quartered, and cored
¼ teaspoon ground cinnamon

1. Once the pastry is thawed, gently unfold it on a lightly floured work surface. Now cook the apples.

2. Melt the butter in a 10-inch ovenproof, non-stick or cast-iron skillet over medium heat. Mix in all but 2 tablespoons of the sugar. Boil gently for 2 minutes, or until the sugar dissolves.

3. Remove the pan from the heat. Place the apple quarters—rounded-side down—all around the pan in concentric circles, also filling in the center. Be sure to pack the apples tightly, as they will shrink when cooled.

4. Mix the remaining 2 tablespoons of sugar with the cinnamon, and sprinkle all over the apples. Return the pan to the heat, set at medium, and cook 15 minutes. The syrup should boil briskly, but not violently. Shake the pan occasionally to distribute the syrup and allow everything to cook evenly.

5. Preheat the oven to 400 degrees. Roll out the puff pastry a tiny bit, just so you can cut out a 10-inch circle. Use a large stainless steel bowl or other 10-inch circle as a guide, then place it on the pastry and cut around it to get a 10-inch circle. Cut 4 slits in the center of the pastry for steam vents.

6. Remove the skillet from the heat and lay the pastry directly over the apples. Carefully push the edges of the pastry down to tuck around the apples.

7. Place the skillet in the preheated oven and bake 15–17 minutes, or until the pastry is a deep golden brown. Remove the pan from the oven and let sit on a rack for 3 minutes. Place a large plate (at least 12 inches in diameter) over the pastry. With one hand resting on the center of the plate and one hand grasping the handle of the pan, quickly invert the pan and let the tart drop onto the plate. Remove the pan. Let the tart cool until it is warm or at room temperature before serving.

Plum Walnut Crisp

Tender chunks of plum simmer in thickened scarlet-colored juices—all under a canopy of clove-spiked crumbs. This crisp is as delicious as it is pretty.

Serves 4–6

2 pounds ripe plums (about 12), pitted and cut into sixths
½ cup firmly packed light brown sugar
1 tablespoon unbleached flour
2 tablespoons orange juice

The Topping
½ cup unbleached flour
⅓ cup finely chopped walnuts
½ cup firmly packed light brown sugar
¼ teaspoon ground cloves
4 tablespoons chilled unsalted butter, cut into bits

1. Preheat the oven to 375 degrees.
2. Place the plums in a shallow 1½- to 2-quart baking dish. Sprinkle on the sugar, flour, and orange juice, then toss lightly.
3. To make the topping, combine the flour, walnuts, sugar, and cloves in a medium-size bowl. Drop in the butter bits and toss to coat with the flour. With your fingertips rub the butter into the flour mixture until evenly moist crumbs form. Sprinkle all over the plums.
4. Bake 35 minutes, or until juices bubble energetically and the top is brown. Cool on a wire rack until at room temperature. Serve plain, with vanilla ice cream, or with whipped cream flavored with a splash of cassis.

Rhubarb Bars

The incomparable tang of rhubarb is the perfect foil for the rich, flaky crust that underlies these sumptuous bars. This dessert would work equally well as an informal treat, or served after a special meal. For the latter, place a bar on a pretty dessert plate and sift confectioners' sugar over the bar *and* around the plate. Serve with espresso.

Makes 20 bars

The Crust

1½ sticks (12 tablespoons) unsalted butter, very soft

⅓ cup sugar

1 large egg

1 teaspoon vanilla extract

2 cups unbleached flour

¼ teaspoon salt

The Topping

2 large eggs

5 cups (about 1½ pounds) thinly sliced rhubarb

1½ cups sugar

½ cup unbleached flour

½ teaspoon allspice

½ teaspoon cinnamon

½ teaspoon salt

Confectioners' sugar for dusting

1. Preheat the oven to 350 degrees. Set aside a 9 × 13-inch Pyrex baking dish, or similar size pan.

2. To make the crust, combine the butter, sugar, egg, and vanilla in a large bowl and beat with an electric mixer until *very* smooth. Add the flour and salt and beat just until the dough is evenly moistened, about 1 minute. Don't overbeat it. Scrape the crumbly

dough into the baking dish and, using your fingertips, press it evenly onto the bottom of the dish. Place the dish in the oven and precook the crust for 15 minutes.

3. Meanwhile prepare the topping. Beat the eggs in a large bowl. Stir in the remaining topping ingredients.

4. When the crust is done, remove the pan from the oven. Pour on the topping and spread evenly. Bake 45 minutes. Cool completely on a wire rack. Cut the bars into 20 pieces. Serve dusted with confectioners' sugar. Cover and chill any leftover bars. Bring to room temperature before serving.

Date Crumb Squares

These sweet morsels were the delight of my elementary school years in New Bedford, Massachusetts. After attending midweek early morning mass by myself, I would have a half hour or so before the other kids arrived at school. This would be the time I'd walk a few blocks over to Worthington's Bakery, in a state of peaceful reverie, and select a treat. More often than not it would be a Date Crumb Square, so concentrated in flavor that I could take little bites and have it last for the duration of the walk back to school.

These squares would make an ideal sweet for a buffet, for they can be made a few days in advance and taste just as fresh as the day they were made. Because they are best cut into small squares, you'll have an ample amount and you can freeze a portion for another day.

Makes about 35 (2-inch) squares

The Filling

³/₄ pound pitted dates

¹/₂ cup firmly packed light brown sugar

²/₃ cup water

1 teaspoon vanilla extract

The Crust

1 ¹/₂ cups unbleached flour

1 ¹/₂ cups quick oats

1 cup firmly packed light brown sugar

¹/₂ teaspoon baking soda

1 ¹/₂ sticks (12 tablespoons) cold unsalted butter

1. Combine the filling ingredients in a medium-size saucepan and bring to a simmer over medium heat. Cook 1 minute, stirring to dissolve the sugar. Let the mixture cool to room temperature.

2. Preheat the oven to 350 degrees. Butter a 9 × 13-inch baking dish.

3. Puree the date mixture in a food processor and set aside.

4. To make the crust, combine the flour, oats, brown sugar, and baking soda in a large bowl. Stir to evenly mix it. Cut the butter into bits, drop it into the mixture, and toss to coat it. Using your fingertips, rub the butter into the flour mixture until even crumbs form.

5. Pour half the contents into the baking dish and pat it down evenly. Spoon the date mixture on it and spread it out evenly with a spatula. Crumble the remaining flour mixture over the date layer and press it down lightly.

6. Bake 30–35 minutes, or until evenly golden. Cool completely before cutting it into 2-inch squares. Store well wrapped at room temperature, or freeze up to 1 month and bring to room temperature before serving.

Chocolate Almond Macaroons

Chewy and almost candy-like, these fabulous macaroons are sure to draw raves. Buttered parchment paper works best to prevent the macaroons from sticking, but buttered aluminum foil will do an adequate job if parchment paper is unavailable.

Makes 24 large cookies

1 ⅔ cups (8 ounces) whole almonds

4 ounces semi-sweet chocolate, chopped, or ⅔ cup semi-sweet chocolate chips

1 cup sugar

Pinch salt

1 large egg, at room temperature

2 egg whites, at room temperature

½ teaspoon almond extract

1. Preheat the oven to 325 degrees. Place the almonds on a baking sheet and toast for 5–7 minutes, or until fragrant. Let cool completely. Raise the oven heat to 350 degrees.

2. Place the chocolate in a small saucepan over low heat and melt it, stirring constantly. Do not let it get too hot. Let cool to room temperature.

3. Place the almonds, sugar, and salt in a food processor and process until very fine.

4. Add the egg, egg whites, almond extract, and melted chocolate and process just until combined. Scrape the mixture into a medium-size bowl.

5. Line 1 or 2 baking sheets—you can make this with 2 baking sheets or use 1 baking sheet and bake the cookies in 2 batches—with lightly buttered parchment paper or aluminum foil. Place a bowl of water in front of you next to the cookie batter. Moisten your hands and then form balls of dough the size of a walnut, rolling the dough in your palms. Place 12 on each baking sheet, making sure to keep your hands moistened at all times. (This mixture will be soft but should be workable with the moistened-hand method. If for some reason it is too soft to form a ball, chill the mixture for 5 minutes to firm up the chocolate somewhat.)

6. If you are using 2 baking sheets, arrange the oven racks so that one is in the center of the oven, and one is *above* the center rack. Otherwise, just use the center placement if you are baking one batch at a time. Bake the macaroons 12–14 minutes, alternating the baking sheets halfway during cooking. When done, the macaroons will have puffed up but will still be soft. Do not overcook them. With a spatula immediately remove the cookies and cool completely on a wire rack. You can store them at room temperature in a covered tin if you haven't eaten them all, but it is best to store them in the refrigerator, then bring them to room temperature before eating. These macaroons also freeze very well—up to 1 month—if well wrapped.

Mixed Berry Frozen Yogurt

I use frozen berries for this smashing frozen yogurt because the dessert is frozen anyway, and they are exceptionally convenient. You can buy mixed frozen berries in one bag in the freezer section of most supermarkets. They'll produce the vivid, fruity flavor that marks this refreshing dessert, along with an irresistible rosy hue.

Even though this frozen yogurt is a snap to prepare, you must start it early in the day to provide sufficient time for freezing.

Serves 8

2 (12-ounce) bags (4 generous cups) frozen mixed berries (strawberries, raspberries, blueberries, and blackberries), thawed
1 cup firmly packed light brown sugar
½ cup frozen orange juice concentrate
2 cups plain yogurt

1. Puree the berries in a food processor. Place a strainer over a large bowl, and, in batches, pour the mixture through the strainer to filter out the seeds. Use a large spoon to continuously tap the rim of the strainer—this will help the liquid shake through the strainer. Discard the seeds, and return the fruit puree to the processor. (I know what you're thinking, "Hmmm, maybe I could skip this step . . ." But you can't; the seeds will spoil the silken texture.)

2. Add the sugar and orange juice concentrate and process until mixed. Add the yogurt and process just until combined.

3. Pour the mixture into a shallow, metal baking pan (such as an 8 × 8-inch pan) and freeze until solid, about 3 hours. Break up the mass into chunks and process them in the food processor until smooth. Return the mixture to the pan and freeze until scoopable, not slushy, about 4 more hours. If it gets frozen too long and is too firm to scoop, let it sit in the refrigerator until the right consistency is achieved. Store leftover frozen yogurt in the freezer in a tightly covered plastic container for up to 4 days.

Cappuccino Ice

Homemade desserts don't come much easier than this, yet it has all the flavor and charm of something that's been labored over. This frozen dessert is technically an "ice"—not a sorbet—because it has cream in it; however, the word "ice" often conjures up an image of something with ice crystals and a grainy texture, and this dessert is smooth and delicate, as a properly made ice should be. The creamy texture will develop when the mixture is aerated in the food processor, creating a final product that will literally melt in your mouth.

Another fun way to serve this is to skip the second freezing that normally takes place after the "ice" has been processed, and instead pour the slushy mixture into tall glasses and serve with straws and long-handled spoons. You have now made "granitas."

Serves 6–8

3 cups prepared espresso or other strong coffee, with or without caffeine

1¼ cups sugar

1 cup light cream (or half milk, half heavy cream)

1 tablespoon Kahlúa (or other coffee liqueur)

1. Combine the coffee and sugar in a medium-size saucepan and heat, stirring frequently, until the sugar melts. Remove from the heat and pour in the cream and Kahlúa. Stir to blend. Let cool.

2. Pour the mixture into an 8 × 8-inch metal pan (or similar shallow pan), and freeze until hard, about 4 hours.

3. Break into chunks and process in a food processor until smooth and slushy. Scrape it into a plastic container and cover tightly. Freeze again until scoopable and no longer slushy, about 1 hour. If it gets too hard, let it thaw in the refrigerator until it is the right consistency to scoop. Serve in decorative glass goblets. Leftover cappuccino ice will keep up to 4 days or so.

Menus

Green Leaf Salad with Fennel, Apple, and Pecans
Fresh Fettuccine with Spinach, Red Peppers, and Smoked Cheese
Chocolate Orange Almond Torte

Spinach Salad with Sesame Dressing
Couscous Pilaf with Pistachios and Scallions
Easy Tarte Tatin

Red Leaf Lettuce with Crumbled Goat Cheese and Honey-Mustard Dressing
Sweet Potato and Vegetable Tian
Nantucket Cranberry Cake

Salad of Baby Greens with Baked Goat Cheese
Spicy Thai-Style Noodles
Caramelized Pear and Ginger Upside-Down Cake

Green Leaf Salad with Fennel, Apple, and Pecans
Polenta with Spicy Tomato-Garlic Sauce
Nantucket Cranberry Cake

Orange, Red Onion, and Black Olive Salad
Cauliflower and Potato Tian
Chocolate Almond Macaroons

Mixed Greens with Pears, Walnuts, and Blue Cheese
White Bean and Vegetable Gratin
Orange Almond Cake

Red Leaf Lettuce with Crumbled Goat Cheese and Honey-Mustard Dressing
Penne with Fried Tofu, Roasted Peppers, and Olives
Cappuccino Ice

Spinach Salad with Sesame Dressing
Noodles with Cashews in Curried Coconut Sauce
Almond Pound Cake

Mushroom Salad with Sun-Dried Tomato Vinaigrette
Baked Cheese Polenta with Swiss Chard
Cappuccino Ice

Spinach Salad with Oranges and Toasted Pecans
Penne and Cauliflower Gratin in Tomato-Cream Sauce
Mixed Berry Frozen Yogurt

Orange, Red Onion, and Black Olive Salad
Spinach, Roasted Red Pepper, and Corn Enchiladas
Chocolate Almond Macaroons

Mixed Greens with Pears, Walnuts, and Blue Cheese
Ziti with Cauliflower, Tomatoes, and Hot Peppers
Cassata Siciliana

Boston Lettuce and Arugula Salad with Dried Cranberries and Walnuts
Baked Pasta Shells with Eggplant
Rhubarb Bars

Spinach Salad with Oranges and Toasted Pecans
Spicy Peanut Noodles
Date Crumb Squares

Mesclun Salad with Dried Apricots and Spiced Nuts
Rigatoni with Potatoes, Arugula, and Tomatoes
Almond Pound Cake

Mesclun Salad with Dried Apricots and Spiced Nuts
Tortellini with Fennel, Tomatoes, and Spinach
Chocolate Orange Almond Torte

Especially for Summer

Tiny Eggplant Turnovers
Marinated Fried Tofu and Vegetable Salad with Mesclun
Cassata Siciliana

Goat Cheese Spread with Pistachios and Mint
Summer Spaghetti Salad
Quick Strawberry Shortcake

Triple Pepper Bruschetta
Bow-Tie Pasta and Fried Tofu Salad with Sesame Dressing
Strawberry Almond Cream Cake

Spinach Dip with Pita Crisps
Tabbouli with Feta and Cucumbers
Quick Strawberry Shortcake

Hummus with Pita Triangles
Soba and Fried Tofu Salad with Shredded Spinach
Mixed Berry Frozen Yogurt

Goat Cheese Spread with Pistachios and Mint
Thai Noodle and Green Bean Salad
Plum Walnut Crisp

Soup Suppers

Red Leaf Lettuce with Crumbled Goat Cheese and Honey-Mustard Dressing
    Sweet Potato Chili
        Wacky Cake

Salad of Baby Greens with Baked Goat Cheese
    Leek and Potato Chowder
        Chocolate Orange Almond Torte

Mushroom Salad with Sun-Dried Tomato Vinaigrette
    Creamy White Bean Soup with Red Pepper Swirl
        Caramelized Pear and Ginger Upside-Down Cake

Boston Lettuce and Arugula Salad with Dried Cranberries and Walnuts
    Chickpea and Swiss Chard Soup with Parmesan Crostini
        Easy Tarte Tatin

Orange, Red Onion, and Black Olive Salad
    Mediterranean Vegetable Soup with Feta Cheese
        Orange Almond Cake

Index